# EXPECT SUCCESS!
## The Science Of The
## Over 50 Career Search

by

Bill Humbert

DORRANCE
PUBLISHING CO
EST. 1920
PITTSBURGH, PENNSYLVANIA 15238

Dorrance Publishing Co
585 Alpha Drive
Pittsburgh, PA 15238
Visit our website at *www.dorrancebookstore.com*

ISBN: 978-1-6386-7300-2
eISBN: 978-1-6386-7648-5

# Praise for *Expect Success!*

Life is all about building relationships and making those key connections. Finding a job is always an arduous process at any given time, but right now, it is even more difficult to get your foot in the door. That connection is your way in. Bill's book shows readers the 'in's & out's' of job recruitment and it provides an insider's guide to standing out from the competition. If you're job searching or thinking about a career change, read this book and you'll be ready for a new world.

*— Jeffrey Hayzlett — Primetime TV & Podcast Host, Speaker,*
*Author and Part-Time Cowboy*

Having worked in the same building for 37 years, 20 with the company that bought us last, I had no intentions of looking for other employment. Without notice I found myself unemployed just months away from turning 60. Not enough money to retire, where do I find a job? I found my answers and a path forward when my search led me to Bill Humbert. He calmed my fears, paved a path forward and put me to work selling myself. Within a short period of time, I had my pick of offers and found myself back in the game. Thanks Bill.

*— Brian P.*

Several years ago, I had the great fortune to cross paths with Bill Humbert. I was laid off from my position with a Fortune 500 company. After working for 14 years with this organization, I was completely unprepared. With Bill's support, I landed a fantastic opportunity within 90 days of starting my search. Ironically, 90 days was the estimate Bill gave me when we started working together based on the level of effort I put into my job search. Bill provided me guidance on getting started, revamp my resume, developing my "elevator pitch," and working my network. What was most impactful was support through the waves of emotion I experienced in my search. If you've been laid off, lost a job, or just ready for a change, I highly recommend working with Bill.

*— Shari W.*

It is my pleasure to highly recommend Bill Humbert as the very best professional recruiter that I know. Speaking from the candidate's perspective, I had my initial contact with Bill just before Thanksgiving for a senior sales leader role for a major international corporation. Bill conducted the initial interview, made several improvements to my resume and presented my candidacy to his client. Interviews from the employers side started immediately and within 4 weeks I was hired. Throughout the process, Bill remained in constant contact and continued to advise and coach me. You will definitely get the best in service should you be a candidate for Bill Humbert.

*— Michael B.*

I'm grateful to have Bill help me through two difficult layoffs. The skills I learned helped me find more fulfilling and higher paying positions, even in my 50's.

— Shelly R.

Bill Humbert *(the RecruiterGuy)* has just authored another excellent piece of work, **Expect Success** — the best of his books so far and aimed squarely at the 50+ age job seeker. My own business is career coaching and mentoring, and I have employed Bill's techniques countless times with my clients. Bill offers a clear differentiator stemming from his dual perspective of being both a Career Coach and Executive Recruiter. **Expect Success** is replete with real life examples/stories to make his points 'come alive'; good To Do Lists with relevant checkpoints along the way; do's and don'ts checklists (e.g., business interview meals); and, Bill's how-to for salary negotiation are all not to be missed if you are looking to make a step up!

— Tom Grondalski — Career Coach

*To Linda,*
*My Loving — and Patient — Wife*

# OTHER BOOKS BY BILL HUMBERT

*EMPLOYEE 5.0, Secrets Of A Successful Job Search*
*In The New World Order*

*RecruiterGuy's Guide To Finding A Job*

# CONTENTS

# INTRODUCTION

O nce Upon a Time, there was a group of brilliant 20-something and 30-something-year-olds, some of whom worked at companies with the names of Microsoft, Oracle, Apple, and LinkedIn. Many of them were managers who knew that 50-year-old workers were out of touch with their generation and their technology. Therefore, they did not hire them. Just as in those fairy tales when princesses spin and time flies by, these 20-somethings and 30-somethings twirled in the January 1 to December 31 fiscal work world. Sadly, they awoke one day at age 50 with some new wrinkles. Then, their company reorganized or was acquired, and they were laid off. They found new companies on Indeed where they applied and the new 20-somethings and 30-somethings in charge felt 50-somethings were "suddenly" out of touch. While they had valuable experience, they were not hired. Their new world was not the same as the one they just left. Yet, it was the same . . .

Interestingly, the transition from a fairy tale beginning to science for your career search is simple. This introduction discusses the Psychology behind some people's decisions. Candidates need to understand how others think to be successful in landing a new position. Additionally, Mathematics is involved with your goal setting, networking, and compensation. The Science behind your search is weaved in and out of this book.

**One of the toughest periods to find a job in a person's work life is when they are approaching age 50 — or older.** I know. I am over 50 years old. I remember how difficult change was for me. Additionally, as an experienced expert executive career coach, I work with people like you every week.

During Covid-19, many companies had to lay off approximately 12 million employees. Yet from mid-March 2020 to mid-April 2020, seven of the professionals I coached accepted offers in one month. What's more, is that five of them accepted offers in six figures and two clients had two career offers to consider. All of these people were over 50, except for two professionals in their mid-40's. Between mid-March 2020 and December 31 2020, thirty-two professionals I coached accepted new career offers, most of them accepted offers above their previous compensation, with one receiving 30% more than her current compensation and another received 35% above his last compensation. One professional in a technology company received an 80% increase in compensation! There are positions open in many careers for many reasons, including sadly, illness and death.

## Why You Should Read this Book to Find Your Next Career Position

1. I am over 50 and have experienced and faced your fears and questions, and successfully overcame them.
2. For 40 years, I have focused on recruiting (specifically, talent attraction) and my business is RecruiterGuy.com. Other recruiters and I are your gatekeepers, and my advice is based on real world examples of how candidates get hired. As a recognized expert, I speak on talent attraction to associations, colleges, and companies across the country. My talent attraction blogs and LinkedIn posts are well-read.
3. My salary negotiation script has benefitted thousands of jobseekers since the 1980s. Based on my recruiting experience, I know what you can say. More importantly, I know what you should not say — and tell you how to avoid the questions, "What are you earning" or "What compensation do you expect?"

It is time, to be honest with you — and know that I will always be honest with you —working to find your next career is hard work! That is okay. I will be with you at each step of the process.

Since we are being honest here, there is another important "truth"—we only use 10% of our brains. Can you imagine how bored the other 90% of our brain is? I believe we can condition parts of our currently unused brains to think positive thoughts instead of withholding information such as, better examples to demonstrate expertise during interviews and tormenting us with thoughts that we will never find another job.

## This Book is for Three Groups of Professionals

1. Professionals actively searching for a new position because they have already lost a job as a result of a reduction in force.
2. Professionals who decided to explore other options because they survived one company lay off and want to protect their career from the second round of layoffs.
3. Professionals who decided to take control of their careers, become independent of the largesse of the company to determine — and often undermine — their growth and promotions. These professionals always have a simmering search — ready to take it to a boil at a moment's notice.

Recently, I worked with a gentleman who began at his company as an intern. When he graduated from college as an engineer, they offered him a job. He worked for that company for the next 33 years. The company had a downturn; he was laid off. Now he was on the street and literally in shock. He was a middle-aged professional who did not know how to conduct a job search because he had never done it before. Fortunately, his company paid for career transition consulting; and I was his consultant. For the first time in his professional life, he had to find a new career. With my guidance, he worked hard to network his way to interviews. Finally, he was able to find a new position where he could be happy. We spoke again in October 2020 and he still was very happy with his career change — with a corresponding bump-up in salary!

If you had been with an employer for 20 or more years and are laid off, you feel manipulated and betrayed. Those feelings are so strong they are almost like a concussion — everything becomes a blur. Then the company, while truly trying to help you, sometimes will introduce you to outplacement assistance for a certain amount of time. This help occurs while you are still trying to grasp what happened; little of what you are taught here sticks. Once you get your emotions back under control, career transition assistance may be a great help because you will find that the search process you used initially in your career no longer provides a successful process to fall back on.

## The Career Search Process

This book is organized by process or step; you can pick it up at any time and review steps that are relevant to your situation. Initially, you may want to read it from front to back like a novel — just to better understand how the processes work together.

Use *Expect Success! The Science of the Over 50 Career Search* as a reference to help you work through each step of the process. Each step has its place and each is important to do well. If a step is troublesome, fall back and restart the process. With this book, you have a system that, if followed, will help you have a successful career search in as little as 90 days.

When you look at the career search process as a series of smaller important processes, you can understand why so many books have been written on different aspects of the search. It is easy to see why so many people get frustrated; they think they are "just looking for a job." But, they are embarking on a process with complexities that will influence their lives for years to come.

Treat your career search as work. When looking for your next position, consistently work 40 hours per week (or more). Prepare every day as though you are headed to your office. Dress for work. Years of conditioning have made this a professional ritual that signals to your brain it is time to work. You are representing Your Name LLC. The time you invest is worth it if you find a career where you can make positive, measurable impacts doing the things that you really enjoy. As you work through your search by using this book, you will see progress towards reaching your goals.

At the same time, your career search presents you with an opportunity to have fun while you search. I enjoy the challenge from my clients when they doubt me on this. Reward yourself when you meet goals or complete career search tasks. When you seriously begin to network, you will renew friendships with people who will love to catch up with you.

Through your life, you have created a tapestry of your growth, experience, skills, family, friends, associates, and attributes. Your career search will add additional threads to your beautiful tapestry to create a formal brand for your value to a new organization. You are, excitedly, building a new life!

This television interview on *Career Transitions in Today's World* will give you a quick insight into your process moving forward. https://www.youtube.com/watch?v=nwAXmbZ1c-uo&feature=youtu.be

---

*Move on to*
**Step 1**
*and get started on*
*finding your next —*
*and Greatest — Career!*

---

# EXPECT SUCCESS!

# GETTING STARTED . . . FIGHT FEAR WITH ACTION!

Alex was 36 when he was promoted to the position of Chief Technology Officer (CTO) of a Silicon Valley cybersecurity startup. Over the next 20 years, his company was sold several times and his position titles changed within each new company. In May 2020, during the Covid-19 crisis, the inevitable reorganization occurred, and Alex was laid off. He was in shock. He knew his knowledge was valuable to someone but how should he find the right company? One of his co-workers (who I recruited for Alex's company) admired Alex's knowledge and work ethic. She called me and asked if I could help Alex.

Several days later, Alex and I spoke. He was in the midst of the grieving process — shock, fear, disappointment, probably some anger, and feelings of betrayal all rolled into one. We spent an hour on the phone, and I suggested he buy my second book, **Employee 5.0: Secrets of A Successful Job Search In The New World Order**, to help guide him through his career search. We discussed the importance of networking, then we spent 30 minutes discussing successful salary negotiation tactics.

On August 18, 2020, Alex called and was thrilled to tell me that he accepted an offer with a new company! He told me that he read my book and followed every suggestion. It took him 61 days to find an exciting new position with a company that valued his knowledge and experience. Alex told me that he followed my direction word for word in the salary negotiation chapter. The result was that he negotiated a sign-on bonus above his acceptable base and stock options.

If you are 50 years old or older, you have a significant advantage over younger workers. Your field and industry experience over the past thirty years is both your greatest ally *and* potentially your greatest enemy if YOU position it that way.

Let's focus on the positive aspects of your experience. In the past 30 or more years, you have contributed to the growth of one or more companies. Your expertise in your field matured and grew exponentially since you began. All experience, even personal lessons make you the professional you are today. This is the tapestry that I referred to in the Introduction. This wealth of experience creates the platform that, together, we will utilize to find a position that provides you the challenge and enjoyment you seek so you can leap into the future.

If you believe your age and experience may be viewed as a weakness, that depends on how you present it. Too often people reaching the "middle age" believe the maxim that companies do not hire people over 50. This is categorically not true. As someone who is 50 or older, your mind may begin to embrace cruel messages that your career is sunk, no one will hire you, and you may as well give up. Of course, that train of thought lowers your expectation to succeed in finding your perfect position. Then you will potentially fall into the chasm of a self-fulfilling prophecy.

Throughout my career, I followed the Expect Success path. In my freshman year at DeMatha High School in Hyattsville, MD, my homeroom and freshman history teacher was Morgan Wootten. You may have heard his name mentioned as one of the best high school basketball coaches of all time. He was inducted into the Naismith Basketball Hall of Fame in 2000. Morgan was even better in the classroom than he was on the court. In addition to teaching history, Morgan slipped in life lessons. One of his little nuggets was "people live up to — or down to — your expectations. Expect them to do well and they will." No pressure, but, since you are reading my book, I expect you will be successful. And you will succeed because you have the background and expectation to succeed.

I am not a Pollyanna. I do not falsely believe everyone will succeed. I do believe when people apply themselves with a focus to succeed, they *will* succeed. We will work together to help you create your focus.

As your partner, I am wearing two baseball hats — one for talent attraction recruiting and one for career transition coaching. Enjoy watching those hats switch back and forth as you read *Expect Success: The Science of The Over 50 Career Search*. Some moments I will speak with you from the recruiting side (and slide the recruiter curtain back to allow you a peek). In other moments, you will see the career transition coach hat pop on. We will work together if you find your experience at a current company unsatisfactory or if you were one of the 13.5 million unemployed professional Americans as a consequence of the impacts of Covid-19 or an economic recession.

## Getting Past the Grief

I have seen far too many people treat their careers like jellyfish. They float in the currents of their employer, bobbing up and down as the current moves. Suddenly, they find themselves caught in the net of a corporate layoff. This is not to say their work was not important. It was — and they were proud of their accomplishments. They were working so hard that they could not see the signs of their company's demise.

In most cases, those professionals' work was producing results, but their employer was not responding quickly enough to changing markets to survive. Many times, in that type of situation, top executives receive their golden parachutes while their former employees just lose their jobs.

Here you are. No job. Mortgage/rent is due. Unpaid bills on the kitchen table — and sometimes, children in college. It is no wonder you are going through the stages of grief — FEAR, ANGER, DEPRESSION, DENIAL, ACCEPTANCE. One of the stages of grief that may paralyze you is fear. Fear you will not be able to find a job soon enough. Fear if you do find a job, it will not pay enough. Fear that company managers will say you are too old without understanding all your experience will help their organization move forward. Fear that company managers will try to hire someone younger at a lower compensation level.

You may feel anger toward your manager, your former company, Covid-19, the economy, the weather, or the United States.

Before searching for a new position, you must master your emotions. You definitely should not interview while feeling anger because that emotion will supersede all other emotions. The interviewer will not know the source of your anger, they just feel it during your interview. The anger may cost you a job opportunity. You need to work and improve your attitude.

In the 1990s, the Chamber of Commerce President of our town in Iowa asked me to coach an unemployed accountant. We met at a fast-food restaurant. After we began to chat, I felt the anger welling up inside of him. He was upset that he could not find a job, that no one would hire him. I asked him how long he was looking for a new job? He said for nine months. I asked what methods he used to identify new opportunities and he said, "responding to local opportunities on the Monster job board." I asked how many interviews he had from responding to those job postings. He said only two interviews in nine months! Then, the source of his anger forced its way out. He said, "Companies owe me a job because I am a Vietnam veteran who is out of work." I replied, "Our country owes you for your service to all of us. However, companies do not owe you a job. You need to earn that job." His face calmed down. It was a transformation in his personality. He said, "No one ever said that to me." Sometimes, it is best to be direct and honest with people. I ran into him at the local Hy-Vee Grocery store two weeks later. He came up to me and shook my hand and said, "Thank you for setting me straight. I started a new job on Monday!" Nine years later, he was still working at that company.

Focus on positive actions to overcome your anger. You may even want to volunteer part-time at a nonprofit that serves your passion. Focus on helping other people improve their lives. Doing so will help you improve your life — you may even volunteer with someone who shares your passion and can help you network to a new job. Back in the 1960s, we referred to this as Karma. You may hear me talk about the universe as we proceed through our book. While your first job is finding a job, there are other times when helping someone else will uplift your spirits *and* benefit you.

Many times, I coached professionals experiencing the pain of depression. They may deny the depression to friends and family members, but these loved ones see and feel the difference in these professionals. My mental storm flags rise when I hear someone who was laid off is in some kind of "funk." They need to understand it is natural to be in a funk — or depression — after losing a job. It is not normal to drop into a deep depression without seeking professional help.

This is the first time I ever shared this story. In 2009, shortly after we moved to Park City, UT, I was interviewed by our local newspaper about why we moved here from Iowa. We discussed my recruiting business and how a competing recruiting firm in Cedar Rapids was allowed to author the sales tax rules for recruiting in Iowa. The result was my business would be required to charge sales tax to clients outside of Iowa for my service. Since many of my best clients were outside of Iowa, my business would cost 8% more than my competition. This tax would drive my business out of Iowa, and after investigation, to Utah. The result benefitted Utah as well. A member of the Park City community named Anne Gardner, who was a financial consultant, read the article. She then reached out to me and asked if I would join her and Ellen Silver, executive director of Jewish Family Services in Salt Lake City and Park City, to help people who were out of work find new jobs. We formed the Park City Career Network where we did not charge a fee to join or participate. We were volunteers. After a couple of years, Ellen and I were the only two original volunteers who met every Monday morning from 9 AM to 10:30 AM at Temple Har Shalom or across the street at St. Mary's of the Assumption Catholic Church. Over six and a half years, we helped more than 108 professionals find new jobs and another 15 start businesses, including the founder of the Park City Culinary Institute.

But not all who participated had a success story. I will never forget one gentleman who attended our meetings for a couple of months and was wound very tightly. We tried to lift his spirits by suggesting different activities to improve his self-worth. More than once as our attendees came and went, we mentioned to the group that seeking professional help was a way to learn how to turn your life around and to regain control.

On one Monday, he missed our meeting. We called his cell phone and it rolled into voicemail. We left a message asking if everything was okay. Two weeks later, his wife called. She told us he committed suicide the weekend before that Monday. She told us not to feel guilty because he was struggling with depression prior to joining our meetings.

You may imagine the impact that action had on his family, including his children. Ellen and I discussed what we could have done differently if anything.

Far too many times people experiencing depression fail to understand that there are people in their family who want to help — but don't know how. Some friends want to help — but they don't want to intrude. Other professionals would be happy to help — but they do not know your situation until you ask for their assistance.

Take charge of your emotions. May I suggest a book that helped me through a tough patch? Dale Carnegie wrote *How to Stop Worrying and Start Living*. One of the many points he makes in his book is to ask, "What is the worst result possible?" Accept that. Then work to improve on it. His book was very important to me in the early 1980s and his message has remained with me since.

Grief is hard to work through. Everyone experiences grief at some point in their lives — loss of a loved one through either death or divorce, loss of a companion pet, loss of a dear friend, and loss of a job that you love.

Importantly, you are not alone. According to the US Bureau of Labor Statistics in September 2020 more than 13.5 million people are working through the grief of losing a job while you are. If you were laid off in a reorganization, you know some of them.

Occasionally, professionals whom I coach ask me how to determine which stage of grief they are experiencing. Generally, they just needed to speak to an objective third party who knows which questions to ask and it does not have to be a professional coach. A family member may be able to help you by asking what you are feeling. Then match your feelings to those stages of grieving.

I also suggest you contact your creditors as soon as possible to let them know you have been laid off. They may be able to help you temporarily as you search for a job by lowering your monthly bills. Believe me, they get these calls all day long. Many companies assist with the refinancing of homes and now may be the time for you to lower your mortgage payments. If you are paying college tuition for one or more of your children, contact the financial aid office to see if they can work out a payment plan for you — or provide a scholarship for your child. Each cost-cutting measure you take will help you feel more proactive and in control when you are feeling you are most vulnerable.

## Times They are A-Changin' . . . and That's Okay

We are truly living in a New World Order. Most of us who are 50 and older are healthier than people our age were in previous generations. Many of us have embraced exercise to stay vibrant longer. I love taking seven to eight mile hikes at 7,000 to 9,000 feet above sea level in the mountains surrounding Park City. Fewer of us smoke. Full-time retirement comes . . . and then goes. Many of us love making contributions to business and our communities and have no plans to spend our days on our front porch rockers.

Because our generation is staying in the workforce longer, we have wit-nessed — and continue to witness — changes in our industries and in how business gets done in general. Technology, etiquette, agility, and the speed of business have gone through substantial changes several times throughout our careers. That experience is an asset. Have you focus on how things have worked best in your experience or are you open to new technology, means of doing business, and ideas for the future?

When I offer career counseling, many times clients seem to be afraid to take that first step into the unknown — that uncomfortable new territory; the blank white page; however, after they begin to experience some success, the adrenalin kicks in and they become comfortable with that area but may be hesitant about the next step. They need a little help moving up the step ladder. If a step gives you problems, that's why I'm here. You may reach out to me for professional coaching through my website (RecruiterGuy.com) if you need professional help finding your next career.

It is important to understand that it is not unusual for people to find change uncomfortable. As humans, many of us do not like change. Our society has been built through the years to be stable. Stability and change are opposing forces; therefore, my goal here is to help you work your way through change to get back to stability.

## Career Search Like an Athlete

According to the Gallup 2018 *State of the American Workplace*, only 36% of professionals are happy in their jobs. Therefore, chances are pretty good that you are or were in the 64% who were not happy but were afraid to do something differently.

There may be 13.5 million or more people who are out of work due to Covid-19 or the economy. The key is to become one of the tens of millions of people who are employed where they want to be employed — one of the 36% of engaged workers. You only need one position where you can make impacts and have fun. Don't focus on negative employment numbers, **focus on finding the one career position that is perfect for you Now!** Those who are most successful in their career searches are the ones who maintain a positive attitude and perform the fundamentals like a winning athlete. Every athlete and performing artist understands they must study, practice, execute, and repeat.

"Many of history's most successful and impactful athletes use positive self talk to sharpen their focus. The 'GOAT' himself, Muhammad Ali famously said, 'I am the greatest! I said it even before I knew I was.' Likewise, those who are most successful in their career searches are the ones who maintain a positive attitude. They also perform the fundamentals of a career search like a winning athlete."

The purpose of this book is to coach you to understand the fundamentals of a career search so well that you become the best-qualified candidate for the right job. You are competing against other well-qualified candidates who may not understand these processes, and that will give you an advantage. If you focus and remain positive, you can outrun the best in the field. You can do this.

Just as in athletics and the performing arts, the people with the right attitudes, work ethic, and proper techniques beat their competition, who may be more talented — **but, not as motivated**!. Job-search fundamentals are essentially the same for all professional positions — it doesn't matter if you are a CEO/CFO; a professional manager or sole contributor; a technology, an accounting/finance, or a sales/marketing professional. Different areas of this book focus on each level of experience but they all utilize the same steps to get to their new career.

> Currently, I am working with a seasoned professional woman who has many years of business development experience. She now wants to contribute as a corporate board member. After taking the time to mentally catch up with her emotions after being laid off, she has focused on her search to benefit companies that need strong board members. She desired to make a career shift from the day-to-day business developer to the strategy developer on a company board. She will succeed because she has the experience, skills, and now, the focus to find for-profit board positions. My counsel was to initially contact board members she already knows and network with them to find a board that needs her experience and wisdom.

## Let's Get Started! Assess Your Skills

Congratulations! You now understand why you feel as you do. You have already begun to work through those feelings because you understand their source. Now let's get started on positive activities to find you the position of your dreams!

While working your way through the stages of grief, this is the time to begin to develop your job-search strategy. Why do you want to develop your job-search strategy now? It is important to begin to claw your way out of grief. Positive action is always the best way to begin to think positively and you can do this work without putting yourself out there quite yet. It may simply be too early for that. I suggest that you take advantage of this early stage by taking stock of your skills. Some consultants call this a *skills assessment.*

This skills assessment is the foundation for your resume, your "Here I Am!" speech, and interviewing. Obviously, this process is very important. This is the most important step that you can take at this time.

Here's how: Take two legal sheets — you need to use a legal sheet because it has lines 72 versus the 54 on an 8 ½" x 11" sheet. Or, feel free to use a tablet, laptop, or desktop. On top of one sheet write the word "Professional." On each line, write one of your skills, attributes, or important accomplishments. An example of a skill for a professional manager is *the demonstrated ability to mentor direct reports.* If you have a metric that demonstrates that your direct reports are promoted 80% of the time (or something similar), remember to add that metric to your assessment. It may also be something as simple as *the ability to organize a desk drawer.* Simple abilities add up to a mountain of strength.

Examples of attributes are *honesty* and a *positive mental attitude.* Fill at least every line on the front page with a skill, attribute, or accomplishment and as many metrics as possible. If you still have your past annual reviews, these are great tools to help you with your strengths because they are written by your managers through their eyes.

Once you are satisfied with your "Professional" list, write the word "Personal" on the top of the second legal sheet. List all your personal skills and attributes. I once worked with a very talented network engineer who baked world-class desserts and pastries. We loved to see him walk into our office with his latest baked deliciousness! This network engineer would need to include *baking desserts* on his personal list. I spoke with him recently. He is still baking and I am certain his current peers love to see him enter the office. It doesn't matter how seemingly silly the skill or attribute is — list it.

One of the skills on my personal list is that I make the best spaghetti in Park City, Utah. (So obviously you can't use that one in Park City!) I know it is true because my wife of 48 years tells me it is so. She would not lie to me. Of course, I am being facetious, but you see my point. It is okay to have some fun with this.

Some skills and attributes will straddle both lists. It's fine to place them on both lists. Keeping an organized garage or closet and keeping an organized desk are examples of skills that straddle the two lists. Can you feel some of your worth returning as you recall these positive aspects of your life? I bet that some memories are bringing your famous smile back to your face.

Now go back through your lists and put asterisks next to the skills and attributes that you enjoy doing. For instance, as a human resource consultant specializing in the recruitment area, one of my skills is the ability to be very effective with employee relations issues. However, this is neither enjoyable nor fun for me; therefore, it does not earn an asterisk. You will not find those words together on my website. No way do I want Google to find me for those employee relations contracts! This example illustrates how technology can work against your career search. I do want to use technology to help people find a **Talent Attraction Expert**. And, if you link with me on LinkedIn, you will see the ways I promote my expertise. More on this later in the book.

That reminds me — now is the time to promote your expertise! You will learn new, legitimate ways to promote your years of action and experience through this book. Modesty in your career search is not good — neither is arrogance. Strike a nice middle ground.

Once you have placed asterisks next to skills and attributes, develop a quick discussion using the 4 W's — *What was the challenge? What were your analysis and action? What was the result? What did you learn?* for each skill or attribute that demonstrates your ability. When you learned a lesson because of your action, it is good to add that lesson to your story; and how that lesson influenced you. Positive lesson example: *I learned it is important to tell teammates my decision-making thought process to help them buy-in to my proposed solution.* A negative lesson can be: *I learned never to do that again! Instead, since then, I _____.* Just stating that a skill (a great manager) or attribute (creative) is a strength, not a metric. My kneejerk reaction is to ask, "As compared to what?" or "As compared to whom?" Besides, people remember stories better than lists because we put ourselves into the story and relive it with you. While you are telling your story, we are picturing the events as though we were there. Tell them what you learned. Finish the story!

One of my skills as RecruiterGuy is to be very resourceful. On Monday, May 6, 2019, I was hired to provide my recruiting expertise for a cybersecurity firm to help them diversify their workforce, particularly in their sales and marketing functions. I had never recruited for a cybersecurity firm in my previous 38 years in the field. What an exciting opportunity to learn a new industry! (Note my attitude.) The industry did not matter. My recruiting skills did matter. My contract was extended twice because of my success in working with the managers to attract top talent — like you, possibly. More than half of my candidates who were hired were women or other "diversity candidates."

Please explore positions in industries outside of your experience. Sure, you need to learn a new industry, but your experience and skills are transferable. Many of the people I recruited for the cybersecurity firm came from outside the industry. They succeeded because they had the right positive attitude about this opportunity.

## Story Telling for Success

Time for another congratulation! You are moving forward through the important Step One and the foundation of your career search is being poured.

You already are preparing for an interview because you have dredged up the best stories that demonstrate your abilities. Most of your competitors will not prepare this way. They wait until they are put on the spot. Then hope their brain cooperates by giving them the best story, and that doesn't always happen. How many times have you reflected on a conversation and thought, "I wish I would have said . . ."

Why is this exercise important? There are many reasons why you need to be serious about this work:

1.  You need to review these skills and attributes to prepare yourself for your interviews.
2.  You need to be able to demonstrate that these are skills that produce measurable results.

3. You need to understand your value to a new company. Importantly, you smile when you remember successes. This lifts your spirits and propels you forward.
4. This exercise helps you focus and work through the other stages of grief and maybe enough to push you through them. These stories create the foundation to renew your self-worth. They reinforce your belief in your abilities.
5. You may decide that this is a great time to go in a completely different career direction where you are using the skills you enjoy — possibly even starting your own business. Have fun at work. What a concept!

When Bill McGowan, a founder and former CEO of MCI Telecommunications, interviewed potential direct reports, he told them not to expect to make a career at MCI. "Join us for five years. Then find another job where you may create direct impacts. After five years, return to MCI with new experience and skills — and make new impacts!"

Congratulations! You have begun developing stories. Your brain is getting excited and will help you remember better stories to demonstrate your strengths. We are on the way to prepare for your interviews.

It is important in the early stages of a career search to be task focused. Every task completed is a success. As we move forward in this book, create a checklist of tasks so you may happily check off completed tasks. At the end of each chapter, I will provide you with a list of to-dos. Feel free to add to my list! Right now, success in any process is important to your self-worth and helps you build a positive attitude. This is particularly important for people with 20 or more years of experience working in the same company because the career search will be very frustrating for them if they are not used to making job changes to improve their career. As we move forward, the processes will require more strategic skills and sometimes multitasking.

Last month, I was coaching a middle-aged woman who is very sharp and would be a valuable addition to a hospital system. She has interviewed but has not yet landed the job she seeks. During our conversation, her frustration finally let loose. She began to cry. While she was crying, she apologized. I told her not to apologize, but to let her frustration out. We reached a signature stage where she moved confidently

forward networking and found a new job as Manager of
Quality for a hospital system.

## Setting Networking Goals

This is the time to work on more positive activities to prepare for networking. Creating a list is very important for tracking and setting goals for your
networking activities. You will need to know whom to call and their phone
numbers. This gives you a track to work every day. I recommend that you
create a spreadsheet with four columns: name, phone number, where the
person works, and how you know him or her (this may be a referral from
someone else). You can also use paper or even a whiteboard. Below is a sample of a Networking Spreadsheet:

| Networking to a Job Spreadsheet (sample) | | | |
|---|---|---|---|
| **Name** | **Phone** | **Company** | **How I Know** |
| John Doe | 435-555-2045 | Ability Co. | Neighbor |
| Jane Doe | 435-555-2391 | Honest Insurance | Co-Worker |
| Irving Milliken | 319-555-9345 | Accountant Inc. | Jane Doe |

This is just a simple example. Many professionals have ways to create a contact spreadsheet that fits their professional needs. Sales professionals may
use their contact software, such as Act! to track and add new contacts.
Both existing spreadsheets or a contact management software system may
already have names and contact information in them that is valuable in this
process. Remember to copy those contacts before leaving the company if the
database does not belong to you.

Did you notice there is no column for an email address? That omission is
intentional. Your contact needs to be over the phone or in person. You may
attempt to reach your contact via text to tell them you will call them. Email
creates contact problems:

1. Many times, company email servers shuttle outside emails to the
   spam folder.
2. You don't always know they were read.

3. Busy people may want to contact you, but your email gets lost in the sea of emails they receive. Occasionally, that happens to me. I intend to reach out to them, but another priority arises that needs my attention — and pretty soon, I have another 200 emails above theirs — and forget. Darn!

4. Electronic communication (texts and emails) strips the tone and emotion from the communication, leaving the recipient to read the communication with their tone or emotion — and their emotion or tone may be very different than your intent.

And the result is that you become frustrated that people do not respond. At this point in your search, the last thing you need is more frustration. Emails are great later after you have established contact and are communicating. That's when you'll make it through the spam filter and, at that point, you may be sending updated resumes and letters. Often, your contacts will forward those documents to the "gatekeepers" — human resources — or the person with the hiring power. They may even forward it to competitors where they have friends and colleagues — good humans are like that.

Some professionals question whether the US Mail is sufficient for sending your resume. The problem with the mail is the perception that you are "behind the times." If you are an executive, not a mid-level professional, who hears about an open executive position, and wish to differentiate yourself without networking, you may try another tack. Overnight your resume to the CEO via FedEx with a cover letter that legitimately details why they should interview you. It is best to be able to mention who informed you about their need for a new or replacement executive. Important that the referral is willing to endorse you; and why it is appropriate that the executive spend their valuable time with you. It is best if that person calls the CEO directly instead of you. This method builds credibility for you.

Recently, I worked with Jackson, a former NASA strategist, as he searched for a new position. He was in your position: out of work and his brain was lying to him, saying no one was going to hire him. I suggested that he write a letter to the president of a university regarding some positions he felt needed to be filled. Briefly, Jackson discussed some of the experiences he brought to the table that would benefit the university. Then he FedExed the letter and his resume.

The following day, he received a note from the executive vice president of the university saying they did not need his services. Most people would have given up. He told me that his daughter was a student and one of three fellows awarded at the university. I suggested that he reply to the executive vice president and mention his daughter. Within two days Jackson received an invitation to meet with the executive VP. Because of that meeting, Jackson forwarded some of his ideas, based on his experience, that may benefit the university. This may have led to a position. If not, he took his best shot — and learned not to give up when there is an objection.

Later, he demonstrated his expertise with another company and accepted a position as the CEO. Persistence works.

As someone 50 or older you have 30 years of experience and many people managed you, were peers, or reported to you. List all of them! Your spreadsheet needs at least 500 names. It seems like a lot of names and phone numbers. But when you begin to network, you will need at least that many contacts because there is security in numbers. They do not need to be friends. The list may contain family, friends, acquaintances, neighbors, pastor/rabbi/minister/spiritual mentor, parents of your children's friends, former peers at other companies, former managers, alumni from your high school and college(s), your banker, attorney, and real estate agents. You need a base of 500 names because people who refer you to someone else are your most valuable commodity during a Career Search. Why? As compared to "cold calls" to people you don't know, calls to someone who was referred to you by someone else are known as a "warm referral."

Look at your LinkedIn connections. You may have more than 1,000 connections on LinkedIn — especially if you include your 2nd level connections. Ask your family to look at your list. They may remember people that you forgot. You do not have to create this list in one sitting. It is good practice to add to it consistently. Remember, many of these people like you and will want to assist you in your search.

If you are a CEO, CFO, CTO, CIO, CMO, CHRO, etc., your list needs to contain the names of consultants and account executives that have sold or tried to sell you their products or services. These people have connections to people in your field at your level — or above. Remember to include board members whose views resonated with your actions. Depending on their products or services, they may know other influential corporate board members.

If you are an experienced manager or sole contributor, your list should contain people who are in sales and previous peers and managers, as well as those former classmates from high school and college. Have you attended a class reunion? Anyone can know anyone and may be influential in helping you meet the right person. Many job seekers have found these class reunions very helpful for their search. Also, talk with the development professionals at your college. They know EVERYBODY!

If you have not already created a profile on LinkedIn.com and begun inviting people you know to your LinkedIn network, you need to begin working on that now. Remember, LinkedIn may not be as important to the people you are inviting as it is to you right now. They may only look at LinkedIn once a month or more. Therefore, the sooner you begin inviting them, the better.

When you invite people on LinkedIn, NEVER use the standard invitation. Mention how they may know you or how you may be related — same company, college/university, or interests. Then ask if they would like to link with you on LinkedIn

However, since it is a powerful networking tool, it is important to update your profile as you move through your career — not just when you "need" to look for your next position. You can find people listed by companies and by educational affiliations (high schools and colleges). You may also join LinkedIn groups that are tied to your industry and associations that are tied to your fields. LinkedIn has become a very valuable tool for both business development and career searching. There is more information on LinkedIn in **Step 6: LinkedIn Literacy & Lunacy (page 69).**

Congratulations! You completed the first step and are on the way to finding your dream career. As you worked through this fundamental step, you added additional threads to your brand tapestry. It is becoming a more significant reflection of you.

Gamify your career search! Set small goals. When you complete these small goals, celebrate by doing something you enjoy. Activities are good because exercise clears your mind and gives you a new appreciation of the small successes — and how they impact your career search.

# Let's review your "To-Do List" before moving on:

- Take stock of your skills in your professional and personal lives using **Descriptive Impact Verbs** (https://recruiterguy.com/action-verbs).
- **Develop a quick discussion of the 4 W's —**

    1. **W**hat was the challenge?
    2. **W**hat were your analysis and action?
    3. **W**hat was the result?
    4. **W**hat did you learn from your actions — good and bad.

**People remember stories, not lists.**

- **Develop a list of your positive, measurable impacts.** Remember a problem you solved -your response-result around each impact, and what you learned. If you still have old annual reviews, read through them for impacts that you may have forgotten. The additional benefit is the annual review is in the eyes of the reviewer, not your eyes.
- **Develop a list of a minimum of 500 names of family, friends, and acquaintances,** neighbors, former peers/managers in your last company and previous companies, high school and college alumni, neighbors, pastor/rabbi/spiritual mentor, banker, attorney, and real estate agents. Look up their contact information in your address book, LinkedIn, the phonebook, or search on the Internet. Remember, if you know where they work, you may simply call the company's general phone number. The beauty of today's technology is no receptionist is screening your calls.

Now it's time to work on your next step. Remember to focus on each step and do it well. Some steps will take longer than others. Treat your search as your business. It is good to use the above list to check off the completed steps. You are building a strong foundation that will improve your career search. All the work you have performed in this chapter is preparation. Preparation for creating your resume, for your "Here I Am!" speech, for networking, and for interviewing.

Work very hard to maintain a positive mental attitude. Your attitude will determine how quickly you find a job. Remember Winston Churchill during the darkest hours of the Battle of Britain in World War II — "Neva Give Up!"

Remember your bookmark? This is a great place to use it if you need to complete these tasks.

- - - - - - - - - - - - - - - - - - - - - - - - - - - - - - - - - - - - - - - - -

*Let's move forward to*

## Step 2 —
## Hang On With Your Toes!

- - - - - - - - - - - - - - - - - - - - - - - - - - - - - - - - - - - - - - - - - -

# EXPECT SUCCESS!

# *HANG ON WITH YOUR TOES!*

Johnson was a young man with a wife and two young daughters during a tough recession. All around him companies were closing or laying off many employees. He was happy to be employed during this recession — until his employer missed paying several monthly payrolls while promising to catch up each month. The result was that Johnson was not able to pay his mortgage and his bank was going to foreclose on their house. Johnson was desperate and did not know where to turn first — and did not want to lose his house.

He knew he had a month to forestall the foreclosure. He looked for and found a new job with a stable company that was able to pay him every week. Then he was referred to an excellent attorney. The attorney advised Johnson and his wife to file for bankruptcy — something they did not want to do. It was the only way to save their house.

They filed for bankruptcy and negotiated with their bank to set up a payment plan to save their house. Their home was saved. Johnson was more successful with his new company than he ever dreamed. Johnson demonstrated his resiliency through his belief in himself, his family, and his talents.

This felt like the best time to discuss Hanging On With Your Toes! Picture yourself with your back to a cliff, like Johnson — and the bottom is way down there! Only your toes and the balls of your feet are on solid rock. You cannot move one half an inch backward. Is this feeling of fear familiar? Now, take a deep breath. Exhale slowly and act confident. You are on the right path. You are moving forward to finding a new job that you will love.

Over the past 30 or 40 years, all of us have experienced moments where we wondered how on earth we would survive a crisis. It may be health, family-related, work-related, financial, or other personal matters. We reach deep within ourselves to work our way through the crisis.

This is Hanging on With Your Toes. Resilience is important to practice when we are out of work. You found your first job out of college, or even high school. You've likely interviewed within your company and were promoted. If you left your company and found another job, you demonstrated that success.

Believe in yourself. You worked hard, made positive, measurable impacts, and hopefully had fun doing so. Every act — professionally, personally, academically, and as a volunteer — created the person who you are today. You are the sum of all your experience, beliefs, values, and love of your family and friends.

Your experience, and the people you know, make you a stronger person than you were 30 years ago. This understanding creates a professional who can legitimately stand tall and proud (well, for me, stand taller — not being someone who is often described as tall). During your search, resilience is important. Additionally, even if you do not feel confident, it is important to act confident. I speak about this in my 110th television interview, Hang On With Your Toes, (here is the link: https://youtu.be/5LlKolCoCMc)

In their book, *Who Are You . . . When You Are BIG?*, Kimberly Roush and Allan Milham wrote "to be BIG isn't about ego, title, or money. It is about accessing your core inner values and strengths. When you are big, work becomes easy and effortless, even in the face of great challenges."

You may have much to learn about finding your dream job and I will assist you in your search. However, in times of stress, it is important to picture yourself as a successful professional.

Your resiliency increases the threads to your life and career tapestry. Resilient professionals find ways to succeed because they expect success. For more on this concept, watch my 111th television interview, "During Your

Search for A New Career, EXPECT SUCCESS!" https://youtu. be/jZi_h5PyJtg

How are you doing with your checklist? It is important to finish the "To-Do List" before getting into the work where you will apply the tasks from Step 1.

## Let's review your "To-Do List" before moving on:

**Take stock of your skills in your professional and personal lives** using Descriptive Impact Verbs (https://recruiterguy. com/action-verbs).

- **Develop quick stories demonstrating your positive, measurable impacts** utilizing *The 4 W's — What was the challenge? What were your analysis and action? What was the result? What did you learn from your actions — good and bad!* People remember stories, not lists.
- **If you still have your old annual reviews, read through them for impacts** that you may have forgotten. The additional benefit of the annual review is that it is in the eyes of your manager, not your eyes.
- **Develop a list of a minimum of 500 names of family, friends, acquaintances,** neighbors, former peers/managers, high school and college alumni, pastor/rabbi/spiritual mentor, bankers, attorneys, and real estate agents. Look up their contact information in your address book, LinkedIn, the phonebook or search for them on the Internet.

Your business is Your Name, LLC. It is good to use the above list to check off the completed steps. You are building a strong foundation that will improve your job search. All the work you have performed in Step 1 is preparation for creating your resume, for your "Here I Am!" speech, for networking, and for interviewing.

Remember your bookmark? This is a great place to use it if you need to complete these tasks.

Congratulations! You are now Hanging on With Your Toes. We are on the way to finding your dream career! Work very hard to maintain a positive mental attitude. Your attitude will determine how quickly you find a new career.

*Let's move forward to*

## Step 3 —
## Experience Excites!
## Here I Am!

*WE GOT THIS!*
*(I am working hand in hand with you)*

# EXPECT SUCCESS!

# EXPERIENCE EXCITES! HERE I AM!

Maria was a 60-year-old professional accountant. By all accounts, she was very talented. She rose through the ranks of several companies to a director position. The Covid-19 recession hit, and her company closed. She was shocked to be called into HR the day before the announcement of the closure. They told her the company was closing and they did not have money for her for severance.

As a director of accounting, she could see the income vs. accounts payable status. She knew her company was burning through its reserves. Despite this knowledge, she was confident the company leaders would find a way to turn around the business.

Maria was in the throes of a new job search when she met me. She did not know where to start since her last job search was 18 years ago. When I mentioned the career transition industry metrics demonstrated 74% to 76% of all jobs are filled by networking, she visibly froze. "I, I don't know how to network! What do I say?"

24

What a great segue to this step on finding your dream job! Before we jump into creating your "Here I Am!" speech (you may know it as an elevator speech or one-minute commercial), let us examine the landscape today.

Covid-19 is creating an interesting spin on your job search. Many members of your job-seeking competition are diving for cover and binge watching television. Their assumption is "no one wants to hire people now." Their negative assumptions benefit you if you are a top performer. (And don't sell yourself short; you ARE a top performer. Remember Step 2 — Act Confidently.)

The Bureau of Labor Statistics report on November 30, 2020, stated there were 15,672,000 workers out of work. While this report may have job seekers naysaying, consider these facts: between March 15, 2020, and December 31, 2020, 32 professionals whom I coached received and accepted offers. One of these clients was a woman who used my salary negotiation script to negoti-ate an offer with a 30% higher base and with a new bonus — and, if it pays out — that would represent a 40% increase in her compensation. Another was an IT Director who used my salary negotiation script to negotiate a new position with a new title — vice president of global IT with a total package of $260,000. Recently, a third professional found his dream career position with a 35% increase in compensation. I say, ignore the naysayers!

Smart executives use times like this to build talent strength in their companies. They are aware that many companies do a poor job measur-ing employee productivity and value. Consequently, great performers are released with other employees who aren't as talented. Remember the old saying, "don't throw the baby out with the bathwater?" This is exactly what some companies do. Then, they wonder why they are losing ground to bet-ter companies. I am willing to bet that you may have worked at a company like that.

One sales professional that I interviewed was a consummate professional. He had EVERYTHING! He began with a software company in July 2019. He met his target numbers for the end of the year. Then, he blasted out of the blocks at the beginning of 2020. He had sales lined up beginning in April that would net him $200,000 in commissions. Unfortunately, his company had a reorganization. The new vice president did not speak with his current vice president before laying him off and therefore had no clue about how the enterprise sales professional was going to blow the top off of his goal for the year. When the new VP told his previous VP that he laid off this person, his previous VP told him he just laid off Babe Ruth. The sales professional's good news was he found a new position with a competitor — and will not lose a step!

Over the years, candidates have related similar stories to me — the Babe Ruths their companies laid off. I know their stories because I found these stellar professionals when they were available — and recruited them!

Think of your search for a dream career as a new adventure and don't get swallowed up in the perceived enormity of it. Simply remain focused on your very next task. I realize this is more difficult if you are over 50 — or goodness sake, over 60! One small step at a time. We are taking this journey together. Ignore those people who say finding a job when you are over any age is very difficult. As you succeed in each assignment, you are moving in the direction of success to reach your final goal — a new career or perhaps even starting your own business using the skills you've developed working for others.

## Determine the Direction of Your Career Path

Remember those people who say we use only 10% of our brains? Can you imagine how bored the other 90% of our brain must be? That's the side that will drive you crazy if you allow it. Just keep it busy doing the batch processing work and ask for its creative help when faced with an interesting dilemma. Here is one such exercise:

Take some time now to reflect on your career. What were the accomplishments that you point to with pride? Without second-guessing, where would you have tried the other trail at the fork in your career? What do you feel you learned throughout your career? What will you share with the younger generation (without pontificating)? You have spent all this time and effort to build this solid foundation for your career over these years. What experience would you like to leverage next? This needs to be your focus moving forward.

I am teaching you the new reality — there is virtually no more job security anywhere — and how to address the new reality. Computers will take more and more of the repetitive jobs from people. If you are in one of those positions, it is past time to learn new skills. As you learn new skills and new software, your self-worth and excitement increase. The world has changed. Change with it.

In the world today, everyone should take charge of their career. If you are not someone who is purposefully driving his or her career, too much of your work life is out of your control. Can you control executive decisions? Not unless you are the final decision maker. Can you control mergers and acquisitions? No, unless you are the person responsible for the decision. Do you control downsizing? Probably not.

What can you control? Your career goals, your actions toward achieving those goals, and your decisions — and hopefully one of those is to keep your search for a growth position on the front burner. Effectively, you are the master of your wealth growth between now and your retirement. You are the one in control of your future — if you decide to exert that control.

## Learn, Apply, Practice, Repeat

Often when I am coaching clients who are out of work in their 50's and 60's, they feel they should be "doing more" at this point in their search. I work with them to help them understand they are in a process. In Step 1, I compared the importance of thinking like an athlete — successful athletes stay focused on positive self-talk. While the right mindset is key, to win championships, individuals and teams also need to perform the fundamentals well. And how do the greats of the games perform the fundamentals well? They practice them to perfection. Every. Single. Day. Chances are that you may have never worked on some of these fundamentals during job searches. Let's practice and do them well!

Remember Learn, Apply, Practice, Repeat. (LAP — LAP). Outside of my work as RecruiterGuy.com, I assisted as a coach with a high school girls basketball team and at a recent practice I told the students, "At the free-throw line, your footwork will make a difference in your shooting performance." Little things will also help you in your job search.

> Two weeks ago, while I was coaching a sharp woman, she broke down and began to cry. She sobbingly apologized. She has 25 years of experience in process improvement, a master's

degree from a top university, and her experience is top-notch. However, she was not hired in two recent interviews. Her frustration was growing inside of her, and finally, she began to cry. I told her it was fine to cry. We turned her frustration and grief into a positive by focusing on her strengths and positive experience. She is now stronger than she was before crying. In our next meeting, she was back on top of her game. She has since started a new job.

Remember, a positive mental attitude is crucial in the job-search process.

You will notice that occasionally I will reinforce process tasks that I mentioned in previous chapters. Since it takes three repetitions to remember something, many times I will repeat important terms.

## Your "Here I AM!" Speech

You may hear your "Here I AM!" speech described as an elevator speech or one-minute commercial. This is key to your marketing effort for networking and for answering the first question generally asked during an interview: "Tell me about yourself." We are creating a statement that will assist you in these two processes of your search. Think of this statement in terms of the Science of Psychology. Your passion and excitement for your position ignite interest in the minds of your interviewers.

Your "Here I AM!" speech consists of four elements:

1. For 30 to 40 seconds (roughly), briefly summarize your career (best if you can add why you are passionate about what you do). Towards the end of your career summary, add one of your top accomplishments. When you discuss an accomplishment, your face lights up, your voice becomes excited, and so does the interviewer.
2. State why you are looking now. Examples are: "As the result of the recession caused by Covid-19, I was laid off with x-number of my fellow employees." Or, "My company was acquired" or "I am still employed but I feel there is no place in my current company to grow."
3. Next, provide another short statement: "What I would like to do next is _____." This helps the person you are speaking with frame who they feel would be a great introduction.

4. Finally, ask "Who do you feel I should speak with next?" This question is the magic question in networking — now you are plugging into *their* network.

Generally, it takes a few tries (preferably with family or friends) to dial in your "Here I AM!" speech to the point that you are excited to give it to a networking contact. Feel free to script it initially. As you present your "Here I AM!" speech, it is natural for you to tweak it given the person you are addressing. Feel free to tweak your script until you have nailed your speech.

Your version of the speech for your interviews ("Tell me about yourself") will discard everything after you discuss your experience and accomplishment. Ensure you discuss your passion.

# Project Your Passion

In the 1990s, I was hired by a startup telecom firm as their Recruiting Manager. During my first week, I met with the founder. He told me, "I am frustrated that I cannot find people who are passionate about what they do. Attract those people to our company and we will succeed!"

Companies search for candidates who are passionate about what they do. When you present your "Here I AM!" speech, your expression and tone of your voice reveal if you are passionate about your work. If you are not passionate about what you do, it is time to reflect on the list of skills, experience, and attributes that you created in Step 1 and gave an asterisk. What careers incorporate most of those skills, experience, and attributes? The answers will lead you to the dream careers you need to target.

November 2001 is similar to today for many people. The travel industry, commercial airplane manufacturing industry, and much of the U.S. economy collapsed because of the tragic 9/11 attack, resulting in many people in those industries getting laid off.

I was contracted to assist 15 avionics engineers in their search for a new career. Let me tell you, creating a "Here I AM! speech is easier for a marketing professional than an engineer.

One of my clients tried to memorize his speech for several days. When he attempted to present it to me, he failed. He was frustrated because he was talented and was passionate about the importance of his job. Those days, we moved past the "Here I AM! speech and worked on other aspects of his search.

On the 4th day, he failed again. He did not realize if he spoke about his passion, his speech would flow more naturally. We were in Iowa and it was a cool, gray November day. I decided we needed a change of scenery (not unusual in my coaching practice). I said, "Let's go outside." He grabbed his jacket — and I did not (big mistake!).

As we left the office with him in the lead, I looked to the heavens and asked for inspiration. The message was, "Just look around." After we walked out the front door of the building and got outside, the first thing I noticed was the temperature dropped. Time to look around. The engineer probably thought I was a little crazy.

Directly across the street was a huge old oak tree with a trunk that was almost three feet in diameter. I pointed at the gnarled old tree and said, "Tell me about that tree's life." His expression told me that he thought I just fell from the top of the tree — wouldn't you think the same thing?

I said, "Seriously, look at the tree and tell me about its life." The engineer smiled and said, "The utility cut a big V through its branches." I agreed and replied, "They probably did not want the branches to cut their wires again. What else?" He gazed at the tree again. "Down near the street, the bark appears that some cars may have hit it." My response was, "Probably did not work so well for the cars, huh? What else?" Now he gave me that "fell out of the tree" look again. He stared at the tree, "It looks like lightning has struck it several times." I agreed. "Would you agree that the tree has had a rough life and is still standing tall and proud?" He was thoughtful, then suddenly the reason we were outside talking about an old tree occurred to him. When I saw that recognition, I said, "Give me your

"Here I AM!" speech. His response was the best speech I ever heard (until maybe yours!). Since it was so long ago, I may miss something but here it is:

"When I was two years old, we lived on a farm. My dad owned an old Piper Cub and we had a grass strip. Every Sunday afternoon, we would take off and fly around for an hour or so. Initially, I was on his lap. As I grew, I moved to my own seat. When I was 9, I set a goal to earn both my driver's license and pilot's license when I turned 16 — and I did. After high school, I joined the Air Force where they made me an avionics technician. Demonstrating a knack for picking up avionics' technology, the Air Force eventually sent me to school where I became an avionics engineer.

"When I left the Air Force, I was hired as an avionics engineer at Rockwell Collins Avionics. If you are an American Airlines 767-400 pilot and look at the flat panel menu, American Airlines and Rockwell Collins trusted my judgment to create the order when items appear. You are flying with my assistance.

"As a result of 9/11, I was one of 800 people who were laid off at Rockwell Collins.

"What I would like to do next is to work at another avionics company where I can make flying safer for pilots, and the people they fly.

"Who do you feel I should speak with next?"

This was the moment when this Engineer moved from grieving the loss of his job to following his passion again. Within two weeks, he interviewed with another avionics firm and was hired.

Your "Here I AM!" speech does not need to go to your childhood. This engineer was different than most professionals. He found his passion early in life. Most of us need to experience life and work before finding our passion. I was 31 years old when I discovered recruiting was my professional passion. My story is different than this engineer — and your story.

Following your passion engages your spirit. Your search becomes easier and interviewers feel your passion for what you do. This leads to offers, acceptances, and new careers!

With practice, you tune your "Here I AM! speech. You know what is working and what needs tweaking. Feel free to write the script and read it (WITH EMOTION) on your initial calls. Eventually, you will toss your script. Every time, I begin a new recruiting contract, I create a script to attract candidates to my client's company. After the fifth or sixth call, I have it to where I want it — and just chat with the candidate about why they should be excited about the opportunity to interview with my client.

## Consistency in Your "Here I Am!" Brand

Congratulations! You continue to make progress on the foundation of your search. Now that you are differentiating yourself and developing a brand for yourself, it is important to keep your brand consistent. It may — and probably will — evolve as you interview and learn more about the requirements of the managers and companies where you are interviewing. Your "Here I Am!" speech and LinkedIn profiles need to be similar. As a professional recruiter, I look at the LinkedIn profiles of my candidates. Why? I simply want to learn more about them. Do they have a brand as a professional (*I am RecruiterGuy.com*)? Is it consistent with what they told me? Does their experience match the experience on their profile? Have they written short articles about the topic they say is their passion (looking for further proof of "passion")?

## Anatomy of a Good Networking Call

This branding should carry over into one-on-one conversations as well. This is how a networking call may unfold. We will start with a "warm referral," meaning someone introduced you to the person you are calling:

*"Hello, Mary? When I spoke to John yesterday, he suggested that I should chat with you. Is this a good time to spend about 15 minutes?"* (If yes, begin your "Here I Am! speech.)

If it is not a good time to chat, ask, *"When is the best time for me to call? If you prefer, I am available this evening at either 6 PM or 7 PM."* Give them a choice, not a yes or no response. When you call them back, ask if this is still a good time to chat? If so, begin your "Here I Am!" speech.

Then ask, *"Who do you feel that I should speak with next?"*

What is your most valuable commodity during a job search? Networking names and phone numbers. Try to get four names and numbers on every call. That represents one day of networking contacts.

Taking the step to develop a strong brand helps you strengthen the fabric of your tapestry. Every step completed builds self-esteem and confidence — and creates a professional who is more in demand by organizations looking for your talents! You are utilizing the Science of Psychology to create more interest in your candidacy and experience.

# It's time for your progress review:

- By now, you recognize that you are involved in a sales process and completed your skills assessment with examples that demonstrate success.
- You wrote at least 226 names on your list of warm contacts (family, friends, and acquaintances). You are working on the other 150 to 250 names (good that you are exceeding expectations!). How about former professors? Doctors? People you met at the health club or during social events? Your list will grow continuously as you network.
- You have listed your accomplishments, beginning with the most recent and working backward.
- You have developed your "Here I Am!" speech. Practice it with people you know well first. It can be as simple as asking, "Hey, I am working on a differentiator for my candidacy. Would you mind listening to it as I practice?" Most people would love to help you.

Now you are developing your brand as a candidate. Our next step is to tie everything together in your resume. The combination of resume, LinkedIn profile, and "Here I Am!" speech is your primary marketing preparation for networking and then interviewing.

------------------------------------------------

*Now, it is time to get started*
*on your primary marketing piece.*

## Step 4—
## Writing Resumes . . . Marketing

*We Got This!*
*(Remember, I am working with you!)*

------------------------------------------------

# EXPECT SUCCESS!

# *RESUME WRITING SECRETS REVEALED*

The Pandemic has turned our world upside down — and then twisted it a little to test our resilience. A client named John experienced this upheaval firsthand. John had been a CFO for an organization for 33 years. The last resume he wrote was in 1987. He was forlorn, laid off from the organization where he was a leader for more than three decades. He did not know where to begin to find a job. He just knew he had to create a resume. This frustrated him further because he did not know how to write a resume in 2020.

We worked together to create a resume that represented his skills, experience, and most importantly, his positive, measurable impacts that made him most proud. Once completed, he felt he was finally on the road to finding a job.

Remember when I told you I would not lie to you? Here is the truth about resumes: You torture yourself to create the perfect resume. You apply online . . . and nothing happens. Many times, you never get a response from the company. Do you know why? In the 2020s, Science has been introduced to resume scanning on a larger basis. Resumes are first scanned by artificial intelligence in applicant tracking systems that are nothing more than simple keyword searches. The applicant tracking systems do not recognize that a singular noun and a plural noun are similar — and your resume gets dinged. My recent #TalentAttraction #Tuesday blog post for executives of companies — "Recruitment Strategy Development Step 3 — Sourcing With Artificial 'Artificial Intelligence'" discussed how the artificial "Artificial Intelligence screened out Top Talent by searching for keywords in the poorly written job description. Funny story about this blog: When I posted a tweet on Twitter to promote it, an artificial intelligence bot latched on my blog title — and the artificial intelligence Twitter bot retweeted it! The bot was not intelligent enough to recognize I made fun of it. So, I decided to thank it for its #retweet and mentioned artificial "Artificial Intelligence" again. This could last Days! Months! Years! The point is that this is the first screen of your resume when you send it to a company — before any human sees it.

Unfortunately, artificial intelligence for resume screening is pretty crude. It includes words from a poorly written job description that could screen a Harvard MBA from the position. If you earned a Harvard MBA, would you include a "high school degree" on your resume? Likely not. If your resume did not use the Exact Wording from the company job description, your resume will be dinged. In this Step, we will address how to improve your opportunity to defeat the applicant tracking Science.

## There Is No Perfect Resume

Resumes do not find you a job. Their primary purpose is to provide discussion points for your interview. This is important information for you to understand as you create your resume. It is far more important that you spend the majority of your career search time networking and growing your network than struggling with a resume that will be read by a human only a few times.

You have twenty-five or more years of experience and now you wonder how many pages of information you should use for all your experience. You decide to look up resumes online. Every single point of information is different. Some say one page. Others say limit resumes to two pages, and yet others suggest no more than three pages. How do you list 25 or 40 years of experience on one, two, or three pages?

As RecruiterGuy for the past 40 years, I have read more than 400,000 resumes. Some of those resumes truly are classics and you will read about them in this Step. More importantly, we will learn what I am looking for in my initial screen of your resume.

Before we get started, take a moment and watch this television interview with Vinnie Politan on his CNN Headline News Show *Making It in America*. We discussed the top three resume       tips — https://www.youtube.com/watch?v=5g-46MiCVOnU  and they are still my top three — contact information, third party edit, list major accomplishments.

> Recently, another professional, Bernie, came to me for coaching. Bernie started with his first company out of high school. He never had to write a resume before he was laid off 23 years later. Legitimately, his resume was the worst I have ever seen. As you now know, that is saying something! The worst of over 400,000 resumes! I didn't want to embarrass him, but I could have given him a trophy. He managed to do everything wrong except getting his name and contact information correct. For instance, his resume was a list of duties in no particular order. We worked and tailored his resume to reflect his work and accomplishments. Two months later, he networked into a new position with a great company to begin his new career!

Far too many people stress over their resumes far too long. Then, they postpone connecting with their network until their resume is done. But, **the perfect resume is never completed because there is no perfect resume!** You may write a good foundation resume that you tweak to fit each job.

> Recently, I worked with a 57-year-old man who is amazingly qualified for many positions — could almost take a dart and hit an area where he would make positive contributions. Instead of talking with people, his preference was to send his resume to company websites — the proverbial internet black holes. I refer to that practice as posting and praying that the right person reads his resume. He received no calls from those efforts. His self-esteem took a bad hit as a result. Learn from his mistake — network your way into a company.

Have you seen the commercial for one of the job boards that shows a fork-lift loaded with boxes marked RESUMES? The job board company boasts to companies they will screen unqualified candidates out while encouraging you to apply through them online. Consider this: since technology is screening you out, do you want to depend on that method to find a job?

# Selling Yourself

I mentioned the following concept in Step 3 and I will repeat it again in future Steps. In the RecruiterGuy.com presentations on the recruitment process from both the career search and recruiting points of view, I subtitle the presentation, "The Career Search Mirrors the Sales Process Perfectly." Something else that few understand is that the career search process is a combination of many sales processes.

| Sales Process | Career Search Process |
|---|---|
| Identify Need | Need a New Job |
| Create a Solution | Create Resume/LinkedIn |
| Source Potential Clients | Source Potential Employers |
| Needs Analysis | Interview |
| Proposal | Offer |
| Due Diligence | Drug/Background/References |
| Cost negotiation | Compensation Negotiation |
| Close Sale | Close Candidate |
| Delivery of Product | Start Date |
| Product Training | Onboarding |
| Client Engagement | Actuate Yourself |
| Retain Clients | Grow In or Out of Your Company |

If the career search process is a sales process, then your resume is one of your marketing pieces. As such, you need to include your accomplishments, especially for the past five to ten years. This is not the time to worry about "bragging," as some candidates have said to me during career counseling. Your accomplishments should include the metrics and anecdotes to support your assertions. If your accomplishments are not in your resume, they will not be discussed in your interviews. Managers are not mind readers. Resumes stimulate questions like: "Tell me about your experience when you doubled the company's sales. Was that all a result of your efforts or did other team members affect your results?" "How did you motivate your team to assist you in your efforts?"

YOU are selling, and THEY are buying. Sell your strengths. Your relevant experience and skills must get into the light of day!

Remember in Step 1 that I recommended you list the skills and experience that you do well and enjoy performing? Then I recommended that you build a story to demonstrate those specific skills? Now is the time to tell the recruiter and manager the story that you built around that achievement on your resume. Make sure you've formulated your stories that match your resume.

Understanding that your resume is your marketing piece will possibly cause further consternation for people who just discovered they are in a sales process. Visualizing yourself "on sale" can cause some discomfort. Do not worry; it is a universal process. This is the time to get your creative (yet honest) juices flowing. If you are in marketing, you may go much further with an imaginative presentation of your resume, possibly even on a video. Ensure all information is perfectly clear! Most positions require a more conventional approach. This is your opportunity to **SHINE**!

So, you sweat all day writing the perfect resume. How much time will an experienced professional recruiter spend on it during their first pass — the pass that will either screen your candidacy in or out?

When I was on a recruitment consulting assignment with MCI Telecommunications in 1993, I hired Andrea, a junior recruiter to assist me. The goal was to teach Andrea how to recruit. When I returned from each two-week interviewing trip, Andrea would bring a stack of resumes to my office to review before our next trip. Since this was before e-mail resumes and job boards, she generally brought me nearly 150 mailed or faxed resumes. On one Monday, Andrea sat at a desk behind me while I read and separated the resumes into three stacks: definitely interested, definitely not interested, and the (painful) take another look (mostly five to seven page resumes).

When I was finished, Andrea told me that she had timed me as I read those resumes. Since I am originally from the East Coast, my knee jerk response was, "Didn't you have enough work for today?" Andrea was the best person I ever hired. Sometimes she had the ESP of Radar O'Reilly from M.A.S.H. She replied that since I was teaching her how to become a recruiter, she needed to know how much time to spend reading a resume. Andrea knew if she asked me how much time I spent reading a resume on my first pass, I would have no clue and she was right! If she timed me as I read each resume, she would have a sense of how much time she should spend reviewing them. Then, she asked me what grabbed my attention on resumes. I told her that I would tell her, but first I wanted to know what she discovered.

How much time do you feel I took that day on my first scan to separate the wheat from the chaff?

Andrea said I averaged six seconds per resume. She informed me that I spent as little as two seconds on some resumes, and those went into the "definitely interested" and "definitely not interested" stacks. I spent as much as 12 seconds on other resumes. Those typically went into the "definitely not interested" and the "take another look" stacks. My focus is on organization, title, and accomplishments. Since that day was more than 27 years ago and was with paper resumes, I like to think I've improved my speed to review resumes since then.

## Get Recruiters' Attention

You have between two to twelve seconds to get the attention of a professional recruiter on our first pass. What are we looking for?

When we are conducting searches, the experienced recruiters know specifically what experience our clients require. In a very quick scan, we can determine if that experience is on your resume. The difference between an experienced recruiter and the artificial intelligence in the applicant tracking software vetting your online resume is that recruiters can see all of the words in your resume and know that **business development means the same as high level sales** — and the software does not. The software is only concerned that your words match perfectly — and few resumes do.

As we scan for that experience, we are making mental notes on the impact that a person has made on his or her jobs. If your resume was not tailored for the position, we are not mind readers, and your resume may go into the "definitely not interested" stack. You must include the information needed to determine not only that you can DO the job, but you also need to demonstrate that you will make impacts in that position based on your previous experience.

There generally are two more scans of resumes after the initial screening to separate the wheat from the chaff. The second screen is focused more on what the person has done, their impacts, potential fit, and how many years were spent in a single position. I'm looking to see if the person was promoted frequently and how long were they at his or her company. The second screen may last 30 seconds. The purpose is to decide if the candidate should move to the phone screening step. The third scan is a much smaller group of resumes — the ones that earned a screening call from me. That scan easily could be more than a minute as I develop the appropriate screening questions based on the job description and the 3-month, 6-month, 9-month, and 12-month goals for the position.

It is important to pass the six second scan to stay in the queue for a phone screen. Given the number of resumes I have read, you now know what my focus is.

## Writing Impact Resumes

The convention in resume writing is to write your resume in the third person, as if someone were writing about you, and drop the pronouns. No "I" or "me." You also write your resume in the past tense, even the responsibilities you have in your current position. Begin most sentences with an action verb to describe your experience. This is a good time to review the list of action verbs here: https://recruiterguy.com/action-verbs. Where can you insert a stronger impact verb in each line of your resume?

> Last week, I worked on a resume with an executive I coached in his career search. His years of technology experience should grab recruiters' and hiring managers' attention. Unfortunately, he began sentences with "Have led" or "Responsibilities included . . ." (Hey, no one ever taught him how to write a resume!). We reviewed his resume line by line and found strong verbs that better represented their experience to begin each sentence. This week, he has three interviews scheduled at top companies . . . even during the Covid-19 crisis.

Every coach who counsels candidates on resume writing has their own prejudices on the format. There is one common essential: Keep it simple and easy to read. If you are successful here, you are more likely to attract the attention of a recruiter or hiring manager. After all, what do they typically look for in an "impact performer?" Excellent communication skills and the positive, measurable impacts you have made.

I have another important rule: Keep your contact information in a plain, easy-to-read format at the top of your resume in the BODY of the page, not in a header. If you place your name and contact information in a header, it is not searchable. None of that fancy stuff like panels/boxes, bullet points/hyphens between addresses, and phone numbers. Why? Today most companies, including RecruiterGuy.com, store your resume in an applicant tracking system. The optical character reading (OCR) software may not be able to understand the fancy stuff (nor read your header), and your resume will go into the manual loading process. This means it may never get into the system. If it does not get into the system directly, no one will read it, you will never be interviewed, and you will never know why.

Several times a year I receive resumes with no name or contact information. While I agree the information on your resume is important, being able to contact you is also a bit of a priority. Your resume checklist needs to include a check to see if your name and contact information are easily found. This is true on your LinkedIn profile, too. (We'll dig deeper into LinkedIn in Step 6.)

Today's world has changed one convention in your contact information on your resume. Today, you may include your town/city but not include your street address. Also, if your cell number is from New Jersey and you currently live in California, I suggest that you change your number to a local number.

> When we moved from Iowa to Park City, UT in 2009, my cell number had been the same since 1999. Since clients and friends had my 319 area code phone number for 15 years, I was loathed to change my number to a Utah number. Interestingly, I did not attract any consulting work in Utah until I changed my phone number six years after we moved to Park City, UT. Learn from me — if you are in a career search and have a cell number from out of state, change your number to a local number. Since my experience, I've made that suggestion to every professional I have coached to a new job. The ones who listened found a new job sooner than those who were reticent to change their number — like me.

This an example of how your contact information may look:

**John Doe**
Park City, UT 84060
Cell: (801) 555-1593   jdoe@gmail.com
www.LinkedIn.com/in/JohnDoe

Make it easy for people to find you in all ways — phone, email, and LinkedIn. As a recruiter, it is easy to give up on a candidate if they make it difficult to contact them.

There are essentially two types of resume document formats. Most people are familiar with the **chronological format** where you list your most recent experience and work back in time chronologically. The other format is the **functional format** where you group your accomplishments together and then simply list your most recent employers in backward order most recent to your past, including dates of employment.

The advantage of the **chronological format** is that recruiters and hiring managers have a better understanding of your responsibilities in each position and when you made impacts on your employer's business. The potential disadvantage of the chronological resume is that short-term jobs tend to stand out more. If all your true impacts are in the past, say six years ago, managers wonder what you have been doing more recently. Try to list accomplishments with metrics in your current or most recent position.

This a sample chronological resume:

**John Doe**
**Park City, UT 84060**
**Cell: (801) 555-1593   jdoe@gmail.com**
**www.linkedin.com/in/JohnDoe**

**SUMMARY:** Grew division revenues 65 percent over three years. Grew division profits 15% incrementally year over year. Secured new government contracts for IBM. Maintained an 85 percent consultant retention rate.

**PROFESSIONAL EXPERIENCE:**

**IBM** **May 2004 to Present**

**Consulting Services** August 2007 to Present
**Director**

Grew this Washington, D.C., division of Government Services Consulting by 65 percent in three years through hard work and client service. Managed 200 consultants in the government services arena Recruited key consultants for contracts with the Department of Agriculture and the Department of Transportation.

- Secured contracts with government agencies where there was no previous contract with IBM.
- Increased division profits 10 percent per year.
- Maintained a high level of retention among consultants — 85 percent.

**Consulting Services** May 2004 to August 2007
**Senior Manager**

Managed 100 consultants working on projects for the Department of Agriculture. Responsible for client contact and client service. Negotiated a new contract to measure IT efficiencies within the Department of Agriculture's Animal and Plant Health Inspection Service.

- Increased profits for these projects by 40 percent over three years.

**Booz, Allen, Hamilton** **May 1998 to April 2004**
**Consultant**

Project Manager for government process improvement projects. Created the first template for a financial process improvement project at the Commerce Department. Developed spreadsheets that highlighted waste.

Led a team responsible for the Census Bureau's financial restructuring, saving taxpayers $50 million in the first year.

**ASSOCIATIONS:** Lean Enterprise Institute, presented at the conference "Instituting Lean Process Improvement in Federal Agencies."

**EDUCATION:**
MBA, University of Iowa, 1997
BS, Business, Assumption University

The advantage of the functional format is the hope that recruiters and managers focus on your accomplishments and not on shorter tenures nor the fact that accomplishments were made sometime in your past. The disadvantage of the functional format is that most professional recruiters know what to look for or ask when they see a functional resume. In my experience, the other major disadvantage is that many managers feel a candidate is trying to cover something up if they see a functional resume.

This is a sample functional resume:

### John Doe
### Park City, UT 84060
### Cell: (801) 555-1593   jdoe@gmail.com
### www.linkedin.com/in/JohnDoe

**SUMMARY:** Grew division revenues 65 percent over three years . . . Increased division profits 15% incrementally year over year . . . Secured new government contracts for IBM . . . Maintained an 85 percent consultant retention rate.

**EDUCATION:**
MBA, University of Iowa, 2013
BS, Business, Assumption College

**SKILLS:** Excellent Manager, Creative, Experienced Kaizen Event Leader, Budget-Oriented Leader.

**IMPACTS:** Led a team responsible for the Census Bureau's financial restructuring, saving taxpayers $50 million in the first year.
- Grew the division revenues by 65 percent in three years through hard work and client service.

- Increased profitability for these projects by 40 percent over three years.
- Secured contracts with government agencies where there was no previous contract with IBM.
- Grew the division profits 15 percent per year.
- Maintained a high level of retention among consultants — 85 percent.

**ASSOCIATIONS:** Lean Enterprise Institute, presented at the conference "Instituting Lean Process Improvement in Federal Agencies"

**EXPERIENCE:**

| | |
|---|---|
| **IBM — Director, Consulting Services** | **May 2004 to Present** |
| **Booz, Allen, Hamilton — Consultant** | **May 1998 to April 2004** |

You have enough relevant experience when you are changing your foundation resume to a resume specifically targeting a **singular company's opening** to add responsibilities, skills, and experience to mirror that particular job description. Remember to demonstrate which skills are transferable. If you have short term jobs, it is proper to give a short reason you left below your responsibilities.

Which format is my preference? Based on my experience working with thousands of hiring managers over 40 years, we prefer a chronological resume. This enables us to see what accomplishments were made — and when. Remember that Top Talent searches for positions where they may make positive, measurable impacts — and have fun.

I like to see your name and contact information centered at the top of your resume (bold for your name is nice). Look at the example above. Then I like to see **SUMMARY:** in bold justified on the left margin. Tailor your summary with verbiage that mirrors the verbiage in the job description (I'll explain why in more detail later in this chapter). Every summary may be different. In your summary, list headlines of some of your important accomplishments — it would look something like this:

> **SUMMARY:** Saved company $150,000 by restructuring the procurement process. Consistently sold 125 percent of quota over the past five years.

You may add more details on your summary accomplishments in the body of your resume in the professional experience area. This enables either the recruiter or the hiring manager to see when you made the accomplishments. Therefore, it is acceptable (preferred) to list those accomplishments with metrics in both the summary and in the body of your resume experience.

> The candidate took the drug test and within a couple of days, the results came back, and he passed. He turned in his resignation notice at his current job and was prepared to start with his new company in two weeks. On the Friday before his Monday start, his offer was rescinded. He would not be allowed to start with the company. When I asked what happened, the company told me he covered up his employment at one firm by extending his end date at one company by two weeks and began his start date two weeks earlier in the next. When I called him, he said his resume writer suggested the change before I interviewed him — that way he would not have to discuss the short tenure.
>
> The client told me they probably would have hired him anyway, even if they had known about the short stint for one job. Their feeling was that if he would lie about something as small as this, what would happen if they had a major issue? Great point! That is the basis of behavioral interviewing. The candidate was distraught because he lost the opportunity to work at a truly great company and he now had no job. His previous employer had already hired his replacement.
>
> Employment applications typically have the verbiage that states you could be fired at any time (even years later) if you misrepresent your experience. Your resume and application experience must match both education and experience.
>
> Tell the truth on your resume — emphasizing the point again!

Then write, **PROFESSIONAL EXPERIENCE:** in bold, justified on the left column. Below Professional Experience, skip a line, and write the name of your current/last employer (bold/left-justified) and your dates of employment (bold/right-justified). Below your employer's name, write your title (bold/left-justified), followed by your most recent position. Then work backward in time.

Write your resume with your responsibilities in paragraph format and accomplishments listed with bullet points. Some books recommend that you bullet point all your activities. Based on my experience you should only list a few important accomplishments with bullet points for each position. My preference for accomplishments is they have a metric attached to them. The reader can see the impacts. Otherwise, in a resume with too many bullet points, your primary accomplishments may be overlooked in a sea of bullet points. Remember, your resume is a marketing piece; you want to directly focus on your biggest accomplishments.

Understand that your information in the body of the resume describing responsibilities is not in bold. When writing a resume, always begin sentences with an action verb in the simple past tense. Never begin a sentence with "Have developed." Begin the sentence with "Developed."

Here's an example of how that might look:

**PROFESSIONAL EXPERIENCE:**
**IBM** **May 2007 to Present**
**Consulting Services**
**Director**
Grew this Washington, D.C., division of Government Services Consulting. Managed 200 consultants in the government services arena. Increased the division revenues by 65 percent in three years through hard work and client service. Recruited key consultants for contracts with the Department of Agriculture and the Department of Transportation.

- Secured contracts with government agencies where there was no previous contract with IBM.
- Increased division profits 10 percent per year.
- Maintained a high level of retention among consultants — 85 percent.

If you have worked with the same company for a long time and held several positions within the company, write the name of your employer (bold/left-justified) and your total dates of employment (bold/right-justified). Skip a line and write your current/last title (bold/left-justified) and your dates in that position (bold/tab right). This practice helps recruiters and managers easily see that you had growth in the company, instead of the appearance of more jobs.

Here's an example:

**PROFESSIONAL EXPERIENCE:**

| **IBM** | **May 2003 to Present** |
|---|---|
| Consulting Services | August 2007 to Present |
| Director | |

Grew this Washington, D.C., division of Government Services Consulting. Managed 200 consultants in the government services arena. Increased the division revenues by 65 percent in 3 years through hard work and client service. Recruited key consultants for contracts with the Department of Agriculture and the Department of Transportation.

- Secured contracts with government agencies where there was no previous contract with IBM.
- Increased division profits 10 percent per year.
- Maintained a high level of retention among consultants — 85 percent.

| Consulting Services | May 2003 to August 2007 |
|---|---|
| Senior Manager | |

Managed 100 consultants working on a project for the Department of Agriculture. Responsible for client contact and client service. Negotiated a new contract to measure IT efficiencies within the Department of Agriculture's Animal and Plant Health Inspection Service.

- Increased profits for these projects by 40 percent over three years.

If you graduated from college, **Education:** (bold/left-justified) would be next, after job experiences and impacts, also justified on the left margin. List your most recent degree first. Then follow below with other degrees (if you earned them) in reverse order — most recent first. In previous books, I suggested that Education would best fall between the Summary and Professional Experience. Today, the expectation is your Education is below your experience.

Remember to put your name on each page of your resume. Since your name is on the first page, the best practice is to use the header for the following pages — page numbers justified left and your name justified on the right. Resume pages tend to separate on a hard-working manager's desk. Many times, I have watched managers shuffle papers while searching for page two. Thank goodness, we deliver resumes via electricity and pixels. You do not lose page two if you read it online.

## Honesty is the Only Policy

**Here is a HUGE caution:** Degrees are the easiest information to verify on a resume. If you did not get the last two PE credits, the college/university still requires that you earn them before you earn your degree. If you lie about your degree and are caught — and most likely today you will be caught — your employment offer will be rescinded, or you will be fired. That's not something that you will want to discuss in your next interview.

> Several years ago, a candidate that I introduced to a company showed a college degree from a major university. When I checked his credentials, I discovered he attended the school but did not graduate. He was one class short of earning a degree. Over the years no one questioned him. Now we were interviewing him for a sales job for which he was eminently qualified (and that did not require a degree). When we discovered his deceit, I asked him why he lied about his degree. He responded that he thought he was "close enough." It cost him a job that he really wanted with a quality company.
>
> There have also been the embarrassing firing of college coaches — George O'Leary at Notre Dame and Steve Masiello of Manhattan College — who lied on their resumes and were caught. Executives who were fired after lies on their resumes were discovered include former Walmart VP David Tovar and former Yahoo CEO Scott Thompson.

This is a good time to talk briefly about honesty and resumes — and tell another story. There are two kinds of dishonesty and both have negative effects on your career search. The first is intentionally omitting skills, impacts, or accomplishments that you enjoy doing and where you have a great track record. Sometimes referred to as dumbing down your resume, this is an omission that may cost you a job because that skill, degree, or experience may specifically be what the company or manager wanted. While there may be times that you want to leave off an advanced degree earned (if it does not apply to the position), do not leave out impacts. Since 74% to 76% of all jobs are filled through networking, include those metrics for discussions with your network. With 25 or more years of experience, many times that experience may benefit you in a new field — like a new app for mobile phones. Think of yourself as the manager reading your resume. How would you feel if your candidate was imprecise, or worse, careless?

Your resume must paint an accurate picture of you as a professional. Not only does the complete resume establish trust with a potential employer, but it also increases your chance of getting the job.

Companies feel resumes and applications are legal documents that represent your background, and as such, need to be truthful. For instance, you may have had a job for a short time, and for one or more reasons, it may not have worked out. Never let anyone suggest that you cover that job by stretching the end date of one job and the beginning date of the following job, effectively eliminating that experience from your resume. That's a lie. Do not leave it out completely; that's a lie of omission. Include the job. Then add the reason you left. Sometimes, companies paint an inaccurate picture of the job and responsibilities, just to get someone on board. Other times the candidate accepted that job, then was offered another position with another company that paid much more. Therefore, they resigned before their company spent a lot of money training them. Prepare yourself to describe exactly what happened.

Check out this television interview titled, "Liar, Liar Will Get You Fired" where we discussed the various ways I have seen people lie on their resumes — and the potential ramifications. (The video goes black for a short period near the beginning while the audio continues, but stay tuned) https://www.youtube.com/watch?v=oXBCodWrirY

## Details that Do not Belong Your Resume

This is very important! **Do not put any personal information in your resume!** The interviewing process is a discrimination process — hopefully, the manager/company discriminates legally. Like it or not, people use all the information you give them to decide whether you are a fit for their position or not. While companies cannot legally ask you for personal information, if you volunteer the information either on a resume or during an interview, you put the information on the table — and they may use it.

> John Doe is an avionics engineer for Honeywell. He is interested in a position with Collins Avionics in Cedar Rapids, Iowa. Jane Roberts is an avionics engineer for Northrop Grumman and is interested in the same position at Collins Avionics. When you look at their resumes, they have almost the same background in education and work experience.
>
> John Doe goes skydiving a couple of times a year and listed that activity on his resume. Jane was advised not to list personal activities on her resume; therefore, she did not mention that she was the president of the skydiving club in Utah and goes out virtually every spring, summer, and fall weekend to skydive.
>
> Both were called to interview with Collins Avionics. The manager was surprised by how close a call it was. Then she noticed that John Doe mentioned on his resume that he was a skydiver. She decided to hire Jane Roberts because this was an important hire and she didn't want to lose a key employee to a skydiving accident. It was only after Jane started that the manager heard that she was a true skydiving enthusiast.

You need to avoid including skydiving, mountain biking, whitewater rafting, backcountry skiing, and other "dangerous" outside activities on your resume for professional positions. On the other hand, include them if you are applying for a position with an outfitter or a company that supplies that type of equipment. As previously noted, the recruiting and interviewing process is a discrimination process. The hiring manager is trying to determine who is the best qualified and the best fit. It is simply important to avoid putting any personal information on your resume.

Some companies will try to access your social media posts (Facebook, Instagram, Twitter, etc.) to check you out. Be careful what you post. If you are very conservative and the hiring manager identifies as a liberal, your posts may cost you the job. The trial law has not yet caught up to the technology. The chances are that you will never discover what caused your value to drop.

You can add your work in associations or voluntary organizations, particularly if you are or were a leader. If you are interviewing in a manager's office and see a service club (Rotary Club, Lion's Club, Optimist International Club, etc.) plaque, it is okay to ask about their relationship with that club. If you belong to the same club but a different chapter, you have formed the basis of a relationship. Ask what their favorite community project was — if that question applies.

## Do NOT Trust Spell Check

Once you finish your resume, read it aloud word by word. Then read it again backward aloud. Read it a third time forward aloud. Be aware that "form" and "from" both make it successfully through spell check.

**I see "manger" substituted for "manager" almost monthly.** Recently, I saw a university advertise for a Facilities Manger on LinkedIn. I responded with this question, "Does straw come with this position?" They asked, "Why straw?" I told them they "were advertising for a Facilities *Manger*." They did not feel it was as funny as I did.

The same is true for "mange/manage," and their meanings are very different. Many other words in the English language match up that way or are spelled similarly — fan/fun/fin, check/chick/chuck, at/it/as/is, bite/kite, meet/meat, hear/here, peer/pear, peek/peak, see/sea, ski/sky, etc. Use the "Find/Replace" function in your word processing program to check for these and other common mix-ups.

Just because you should not rely on spell check, doesn't mean you shouldn't use it at all. One candidate wrote in a cover letter that he was a "detale oriented professional" (does Detale hurt?).

Once you are totally satisfied it is perfect, ask someone who did not help you write your resume to edit it for you. Since they were not involved in writing your resume, most times the incorrect spelling will pop out to them. It is critical to read your resume aloud again as an editor. Only then is it almost safe to give to a company. Your resume is your representation of you; you are selling your skills and talents. If it is written carelessly, this reflects your work.

In the spring of 1994, I was asked to present the recruitment process to 16 international businesspeople at a northern Virginia university. They were from oil companies in southern Russia. Prior to the Soviet Union splitting apart, a central bureau matched candidates with companies. Candidates had no interviews, no tour, no decision. When the bureau told you to report to a company, that is where you worked. The companies were on the other side of this same coin. There was no interviewing process. They took the person the central bureau sent. They did not need to attract candidates. There were no recruiters. They picked up the phone and called the bureau — and people reported on Monday.

After the U.S.S.R shrank to become Russia again, those companies now needed to learn to compete for candidates and learn how to select the best candidates. That is why they were in northern Virginia that day. I coached them through an interpreter.

When we discussed resumes, I told the businesspeople that "a resume should be the perfect reflection of a candidate's work. If there is a typo in their resume, . . . ." (with that I scrunched up a piece of paper and used a hook shot to toss it into the trash can). It was fun to watch their eyes follow the ball of paper into the trash can, then glance back quickly at the interpreter who translated what I said . . . then, they all laughed.

# Speak Their Language

I once received a cover letter from a candidate that stated he "would be a good fit for MCI" (my client). Then he wrote that companies such as Boeing (instead of MCI) need professionals who understood marketing — and then proceeded to use two more company names in place of MCI. I can't imagine that he was successful in attracting an interview with that letter! This story further emphasizes the need to edit and read all communications with a potential employer.

When you write a resume, it is best to understand that its purpose is to **become a foundation for future resumes.** Before you apply to a company, **change words in your resume to reflect the verbiage in the company's job description.** For instance, perhaps in your resume, you were called a buyer at your last company. When you read the job description, it was almost a perfect match for your "buyer" position, but their title is "purchasing agent." Then they used "purchased" instead of "bought." Change your words to match their words. Speak their language!

Save your new resume for a specific company with the name of the company and date in the file name. Save each resume version moving forward. Leave a paper trail for yourself to build on in the future. First, you need to know which resume to take with you on an interview. Then, you can track what worked and what didn't. Always make changes and updates that list the same work but use different descriptive action verbs (simple past), nouns, and adjectives.

Why go through this effort? Recruiters tend to take keywords from their job descriptions and job postings to search the resume database in their applicant tracking system (ATS). If they choose "purchased" as one of their keywords and you wrote "bought," chances are pretty good that your resume will not be selected; therefore, it is best to make those changes before forwarding your resume. This practice will move your resume closer to the top of the applicant tracking system prospect list because it perceives that you SPEAK its language. There is a software you may purchase that helps you with the resume word match with the job description — https://www.jobscan.co/register.

Think of the applicant tracking system as a Labrador Retriever. When the recruiter types in a few keywords, it is like showing the rawhide bone to the dog. Then they click "search" in the ATS. The computer gets all excited just like a Retriever, and when it returns in a couple of seconds (not like the dog . . .), it shows its excitement by saying in the results that it is 90 percent sure this person is a good match. It will say another candidate's resume is a 70% match and a third candidate's resume is a 50% match. Trust me — the 70 % and 50% match are never opened. Its determination that a candidate is a good match comes from seeing the search words (keywords) multiple times in your resume.

In my 113th television interview, I call it artificial "Artificial Intelligence". This is the link to the interview — https://www.youtube.com/watch?v=0_Z55vgnBZ8&t=22s.　ATS's daily screen out Top Talent because their resumes do not match the verbiage in the job description.

**This is the "RecruiterGuy Hack:"** If you are replying to an Internet posting, save another copy of your resume under the "company's name and keywords." At the bottom of that resume, type "Keywords:" and then list all potential keywords (and variations of the words — plural, past tense) from their job description where you have that experience. Raise the hits on the ATS system by demonstrating you have the right experience for the job. That's why applicant tracking systems will not replace humans in the search process . . . soon. Anyone can add words; humans judge their veracity.

Every company has its own culture and focus. In your research for prospective employers, go to every page on their website and get a sense of their priorities. If they have community service pages, read them because it gives you a sense of their social responsibility. More importantly, you may already volunteer at one or more of the charities they sponsor. If so, ensure you add them to the resume you prepare for that company. This practice demonstrates that you already participate in the community of a company.

Developing an effective resume is important for creating an interesting interview. With your years of experience to draw from, examining the job description will help you create stories that demonstrate your expertise. These stories create an interesting interview because they tend to generate give and take with the Hiring Manager. Ensure that you refer to these accomplishments and experience in your resume. The candidates who work to create five interesting interviews are the ones who generally receive offers because their confidence will be evident in their reactions to the interview questions. Remember to lead sentences with a strong verb — and remember that "led" is the past tense of "lead." Take time now to create your resume. This is a process. To be successful, let's lay a good foundation and then move forward.

## What is the Role of Cover Letters?

Most recruiters who have been in the business for a long time do not read cover letters. Unless I am trying to get a sense of a candidate's writing style, I do not read cover letters either. There is no guarantee a candidate even wrote the cover letter. Many resume writers or career counselors either write the resume and letter or counsel the person on what and how to convey information. If the company requires a cover letter, compose a succinct one. Include the information required and request an interview: do not waste anyone's time. Including your own.

## Do Not Wait to Update

Where do the people who take charge of their careers fit into this Step on resumes? Most people wait until they *need* an updated resume. During the last day of each quarter, the professionals who are Top Talent create a habit to review their resumes. If they need to add a new skill, experience, or accomplishment, they update their resume now. They may even tweak their resume now to better fit a new direction in their career. This habit enables you to be light on your feet to change career direction instantly when the opportunity presents itself. This is a prime reason to take charge of your career! You have the experience. Exhibit it in your best possible light!

May I offer one final resume thought? Personally, I despise writing MY resume. I feel your pain. It is something almost all of us need to compose. Mine is updated every time a recruiting contract is completed with the accomplishments included — do not want to forget them. Follow Nike's saying, "Just Do It!' Then you may move to more strategic aspects of your search.

Remember the Applicant Tracking System science. If the system feels you do not speak the company's language, you will not receive a high enough score to be selected for an interview — frustrating, I know.

Think of the positive, measurable impact that you made by creating a resume that attracts the attention of professional recruiters and executives. This is a time to celebrate your success. Find something that you enjoy and spend time refreshing your mind and spirit. You deserve the quick break. As you complete each step, celebrate your success!

**With your years of experience and growth, you have So Much Skill, Experience, and Attributes to give to your next employer!**

**This chapter is so important that we have two checklists — the Resume Checklist and the Career Search Process Checklist.**

# Resume Checklist

Is the information on your resume accurate? Honesty is the only policy.

- ☐ Is your name and contact information easily found in the body of your resume (not the header)?
- ☐ Are your degree and graduation date accurate?
- ☐ Did you write your resume in the third person, simple past tense?
- ☐ Did you drop the pronouns and begin your sentences with action verbs? (See Resume Action Verbs and Phrases — RecruiterGuy)
- ☐ Did you discuss your most recent experience first followed chronologically by previous experience?
- ☐ Did you include all the measurable impacts on your resume? Remember, recruiters are looking for metrics to understand the level of impact.
- ☐ Have you read your resume aloud? Did you run spell check? Did you run "Find/Replace" for words like *mange, manger, from,* and *form*?
- ☐ Has a friend or associate read your resume as an editor? Did they look at spelling and grammar?
- ☐ Have you saved your resume in your word processing software? Did you print it — just in case?
- ☐ Did you save your resume with the name of the company where you applied and use their verbiage for the position?
- ☐ Did you apply the "RecruiterGuy Hack?"
- ☐ If a cover letter is required, have you composed one that is succinct and covers all the information required by the company?

**Congratulations! Creating a strong foundation resume is a huge accomplishment that you may leverage in your search!**

After you have completed this checklist, let's move to your career search checklist. Think of RecruiterGuy.com as your career search project manager as he sits on your shoulder rooting you on to success.

# Career Search Process Checklist

- ☐ Review your list of professional and personal skills to see if you can improve the impact verbs. Only use words that you use in normal conversation. It's very embarrassing to use the wrong verb.

☐ Review the examples of the situations that required your skills. After thinking about your examples over the last few days, are there better examples that you can use? Again, the format is to discuss your action in the situation; tell a story around the skill. Then discuss what happened because of your influence or direct action. **People remember stories, not lists.**

☐ Develop a list of your positive, measurable impacts over the past 10 years, with a focus on the last five years. List them from the most recent impacts backward. Develop The 4 W's — What was the challenge? What were your analysis and action? What was the result? What did you learn?

☐ If you still have old annual reviews, read them for impacts that you may have forgotten. Create your stories around the most important impact.

☐ Review and add to your list of 500 names of family, friends and acquaintances, neighbors, former peers/managers in your last company and previous companies, high school and college alumni, pastor/rabbi/spiritual mentor, banker, attorney, real estate agents, professors, doctors, and acquaintances from the health club. Look up their contact information in your address book, the phonebook, or search for them on the Internet.

☐ Join LinkedIn and invite everyone you feel can help you — and who you can help somewhere. Remember, it is important to give. When people accept your invitation, go through their network, and see if there may be contacts you forgot to enter on your list. Please understand their time frame and priorities may not be the same as yours. Some people only look at their LinkedIn invitations once a quarter or once per year — when they are catching up. This action may help you remember additional people to add to your spreadsheet. Remember, people know other people — and LinkedIn is a great example of how it can work.

☐ Develop your "Here I Am!" speech. Continue to practice it with people you know well first. Your request may be as simple as, "Hey, I am working on a differentiator for my candidacy. Would you mind listening to it as I practice?" Most people would love to help you.

You are developing your brand as a candidate. Your foundation resume is completed. The combination of resume, LinkedIn profile, and "Here I Am!" speech is your primary marketing preparation for networking and then interviewing. Through the tools you created, you become your brand — and your brand reflects you.

Creating a resume adds more thread to your brand tapestry. Your tapestry is beginning to truly illustrate your skills and experience. It is strengthening your story.

If you have not completed all these steps, put your bookmark back in here, and finish these processes. Remember, these are the fundamentals that will help you find your next job. Skating only extends your career-search process. You have great experience to discuss. Reflect on your experience, your impacts, and the people that you impacted throughout your work — both professional and volunteer work.

## One More Thought: Are You Your Next Boss?

Let's pause here for a second. As you have been preparing your search, have you considered starting your own business? If you have, many community colleges bring business people in to conduct classes on entrepreneurship and start-ups. Additionally, you should contact the Small Business Administration (SBA) to discuss the process. Read some of the countless great books on the subjects and find mentors among the many people who successfully started and run a business.

> Recently, in October 2020, I worked with a professional who decided to retire after 40 years with a railroad company. His goal was to become a railroad consultant. What was holding him back? He never in his life created a resume. He diligently listened to my coaching. His first shot at creating a resume was amazingly on target. We spent one more meeting to tweak it and discuss networking into contracts. We discussed how to demonstrate he is a consultant versus an employee (own office and office expenses, more than one source of revenue, office equipment, separate bank account for his business, pay quarterly taxes, responsible for dictating his own work hours, etc.) The following week, a company called him and hired him to work on a contract for them.

Congratulations on finishing your resume — for now! (You will add and delete words, phrases and add new words and phrases to replace your originals, depending upon the company that is interested in you)

--------------------------------------------------------------

*Let's attack the next important Step —*

# STEP 5 —
# You Got This!

--------------------------------------------------------------

# EXPECT SUCCESS!

# *YOU GOT THIS!*

Our minds can be cruel to us. Recently, I coached a professional who graduated from Cornell University with a degree in economics. He had years of experience with several companies that you would recognize and respect. Yet, he questioned his knowledge and experience. He is not alone. Many people I coach experience those feelings. With his years of education and experience, he should exude confidence! As we worked on his resume, his LinkedIn profile, and practiced interviewing, I pointed out the reasons he should be more confident in his experience and skills. Once he truly understood his value, his next interview resulted in an offer on the spot from a major Seattle Employer. He was able to negotiate a sign-on bonus and an extra week of PTO. His excitement when he called to tell me he accepted a great offer was palpable!

Without understanding the Science of Psychology, some people may cringe when informed that understanding basic psychology benefits you in many ways during a career search. The Science of Psychology studies human behavior through behavioral research. Simply, this research is focused on your brain and how it reacts to different circumstances (i.e. our instinct to fight or flee), how you learn (cognitive abilities), solve problems, and how you communicate within yourself and with others.

The Science of Sociology is the study of group interaction and communication. You may have heard a company describe its culture. Have you seen or heard that a position requires the ability to build consensus or build a team? This is the Science of Sociology at work.

And you thought you were simply looking for a new career!

Our minds are wonderful! It is hard to believe how many snippets of songs that we remember back to our youth. Our minds may be powerful tools for our job searches *IF* we unleash them for that purpose. Experienced professionals so often allow the negative power of our brains to create questions about our abilities to find an exciting, new position. That power creates fear that we will never find another great job. You have the power to control your mind by focusing on the positive aspects of your search. Our minds do what we ask.

We've covered a lot of information in the past four Steps. You have put so much preparation time into this effort; you no doubt long for tangible results to demonstrate YOUR time and effort. It is natural for you to feel a little upset if you've had a lack of results so far. Now is the time to use your power and confidence developed by all of those years of positive experience and accomplishments to drive your search forward!

As an executive career transition coach, my experience demonstrated that at this point, some people are beginning to experience some frustration. Part of the frustration is the nature of the process and the other part is the fact that many professionals are transaction motivated — if I do this, I receive that (money, recognition, promotions). This is the best time to practice self-motivation — no one is telling you what to do when.

## Visualize Success

Just as in athletics and the performing arts, much of this process requires a proper mental attitude and preparation. I realize you are tired of hearing attitude, attitude, attitude. At this point, you are still experiencing the grieving process. Therefore, your mind is telling you things that are not true. Watch for these voices. Your value to a company is enormous; past layoffs are the result of forces out of your control. With each successful step of this process, you'll find your power returning. You will act for yourself — and that feels great!

At the age of 52 in 2001, I was diagnosed with renal cell cancer on my kidney. It was miraculous that it was discovered when it was so very early. I give credit to my guardian angel.

My kidney surgery was on December 21. After my four-and-a-half-hour surgery, the nurses had me up on my feet and walking within five hours. They told me I would be able to leave the hospital sooner if I walked now. The surgery was major, but I am coachable. Therefore, with my pole with anesthesia and meds, I took off down the hall many times (I can only imagine that sight) with my goal of leaving the hospital on Christmas — remember challenging and yet attainable goals?

In the middle of the first night, those voices began chirping in my head. The voices were saying, "Your cancer is worse than they told you. You will die soon. The doctors just want you to have a nice, last Christmas." My wife was working as a Surgical ICU Nurse in the hospital that night. I found her in another unit. She reassured me that the doctors were telling me the truth. My strong motivation was to spend Christmas with my wife and daughters (and spend time watching some college football bowl games as I napped and recovered in the familiar confines of home). I was discharged on Christmas Day. I am convinced the reason was I visualized being home for Christmas. As you may have noticed, the doctors were telling the truth. Those darn voices were causing me concern, but they were not reality.

You may hear the same voices in your job search. They create fear by telling you that you will never find a job as good as the last one. Your voices may say it is useless to do this preparation — and for what reason? Your voices may question the time you put into the preparation, saying you are wasting your time, instead of "looking for a job." Your brain tells you that you don't know how to network (you have been networking since you were a young child, "Where did ya get dat?") I know because I have heard those words from executives I coached. Nearly everyone at least briefly hears those voices . . . until they take control and dismiss them.

This is a great time to practice the power of visualization. Let's get your inner voices focusing on the positive. You have the power of changing the channel and viewing a more positive conclusion — finding that perfect career where you make impacts, have fun and receive recognition and higher compensation.

Visualization is a force so powerful that many of us don't understand until we experience it. Our brains can accomplish our dreams — if we train and believe. Call it confidence, call it faith, call it assurance. Whatever you call it when you are confident of success, most times you succeed. Remember the science of psychology. Research demonstrates the power of visualization.

How do you become more confident? You practice — you visualize success. How many times? All your life, no matter what you face.

For almost 20 years, I coached 7th and 8th grade girls' basketball in Maryland and Iowa, and high school in Park City, UT. One 8th grade team heard my mantra and believed it: "Free throws win games!" Every evening I would end our practice by saying this, "Tonight, before you go to sleep, picture yourself at the free throw line. Look up at the scoreboard. We are down one point. You have two free throws. There are two seconds left on the clock. If you make both free throws, we win by one point. Picture the fans behind the basket waving their hands and screaming at you to miss your shot. Picture the referee holding the ball waiting for you to set. Once you are ready, picture the bounce pass as it comes into your hands. Feel your confidence as you dribble the ball a couple of times. Then with your knees bent, elevate to your tiptoes as you release the basketball in a perfect arc to the basket. Wave to the basketball as you release it to give it a nice backspin. Picture 'all net' as the ball floats through the net and you score!

Does this actually work? You be the judge. With this one 8th grade girls' basketball team, our last tournament was a three-game tournament. We hit 90% at the free throw line and won each game in sudden death overtime . . . with a good free throw. Free throws win games — and *visualization works!*

Picture yourself in your work environment, as best you can. Include every detail you can. If you are an executive, visualize your favorite success story

(Science of Psychology). Why were you successful? How do you replicate that success in the future? If you are a project manager, visualize yourself building consensus with the team you are supporting (Science of Sociology). Take time to "practice" by visualizing every step of a perfect project that you led. If you are a surgeon, visualize a perfect surgery. If you are a teacher, visualize yourself engaging your class to learn and desire more knowledge. Then, if you have a company you are targeting, picture yourself already working there, making positive, measurable impacts — and having fun (because that's important too!). Keep that vision in your mind. Picture it every morning and every evening. Give your brain something with a positive focus!

## Return to the Process Reinvigorated

Remember, the job search is a sales process that requires preparation. The process requires practice. It is no different than athletes practicing a drill over and over again or musicians practicing a chorus over and over again until it is perfect. The most prepared candidates who have the required skills are the first hired. Every Step that you worked through to this point is an important Step:

1. Worked through your grief.
2. Listed your skills and attributes.
3. Created stories that demonstrate your skills and attributes — and improve your stories
4. Created your networking contact spreadsheet with at least 500 names. (I keep wanting to make it 1,000 names but I want you to list your first 500. Then using LinkedIn and other tools, expand your list to 1,000 people.) In Step 8 *Newly Networking*, I interviewed five people to demonstrate how networking benefits everyone, including the CEO of a company.
5. Set your goal for the job you desire and when you want to be in that position. This step is important because it helps you measure your activity.
6. Developed your Hear I Am! Speech.
7. Developed your resume.

**Congratulations!** This is a lot of work that you accomplished. You have successfully prepared yourself to catapult your way through the last Steps to find your job. Rewarding your mind for tasks accomplished is a way to gamify those tasks. For example, when I wrote *RecruiterGuy's Guide To Finding A Job* in 2010, I set a goal to write from 7 AM to 12 noon. Then, I dressed in my ski clothes (we lived at the base of Canyons Village at Park City Mountain Resort in Park City, Utah). I rewarded myself by skiing for three hours in the afternoon. Afterward, as I cooled down, I began to write again.

Take a moment to celebrate your preparations too! Set goals to accomplish different tasks using SCAMPS (**S**pecific and Strategy to accomplish, **C**hallenging, **A**ttainable, **M**easurable, **P**ublic, and **S**pecific end date). Then identify something that you enjoy doing and put a time limit on it. That becomes your reward and makes the work more inviting.

Too often, experienced professionals just want to take some time off. I understand. When you are going through the grieving process, and assessing your desires for the future, it is good to take some time for a fresh look at your career. But now is the time to act. Your benefit will be the success to find a career you love with a great company within 90 days or so, depending on the balance of your efforts.

You have valuable experience and skills honed over your years of experience to contribute to the growth of a company. Mentally prepare yourself to provide your knowledge, skills, and experience to help your new company succeed. You are adding more threads to your tapestry.

Remember the value of understanding the Science of both Psychology and Sociology. We will discuss them further in future Steps.

Visualization strengthens the threads of the tapestry of your experience.

Now, let's get on with the work at hand. Our next process teaches you how to think like a detective to uncover those "hidden jobs" and how to find networking contacts you forgot you know.

In the spirit of visualization, every morning when you are preparing for your day, and every evening before bed, stand in front of the mirror. Look at yourself and smile confidently. Then say aloud . . .

----------------------------------------

## I Am A Professional!
## I GOT THIS!

----------------------------------------

Use visualization in your preparation to network. Visualize using your Here I Am Speech with a member of your network. Visualize them asking, "Are you interviewing with us?" Visualize the hiring manager excited to meet you and ultimately extending you a great offer that you excitedly accept! If you network faithfully, and practice visualization, you improve your chances of finding a job much sooner. Is it worth trying? What do you have to lose? Once you find your new position, continue to practice visualization in your work and personal lives. Teach your mind your new way to think and prepare!

- - - - - - - - - - - - - - - - - - - - - - - - - - - - - - - - - - - - - - - - - - - - - - -

*YOU GOT THIS!*

*Now let's learn*
**LinkedIn Literacy**
*(and possibly, some Lunacy)*
*in* **STEP 6***!*

- - - - - - - - - - - - - - - - - - - - - - - - - - - - - - - - - - - - - - - - - - - - - - -

## STEP 6

# LINKEDIN LITERACY & LUNACY

Many professionals in their late 50s and early 60s never developed a LinkedIn profile because they thought they would retire with the company where they worked the past 15 years. Emily was one of those people. She was a successful manager for a technology firm. The company was very successful and profitable. Over time, their success was noticed by larger firms. Finally, one of those firms acquired Emily's firm. Many times, the acquiring firm reassures employees of their recently acquired company that they have nothing to fear. Their jobs are safe. But, if they tell investors they will take advantage of synergies, it means people will lose their jobs. Emily was one of those people. She believed her job was safe — and it was not. In the first wave of the reduction in force, Emily was one of 250 employees who lost their jobs.

Emily was distraught. She felt she was safe and in ten years she would retire from her company. She had a LinkedIn profile because one of her children bugged her until she created it. "There! It is done!" Unfortunately, it was not created in a way that would attract other professionals who may be searching for someone with Emily's skills.

When we met, Emily began to cry. She heard that companies did not hire people over 50 (oh yes, they do!). She was too young to retire. She did not know where to begin. I coached her through our initial 5 Steps and then we focused on her LinkedIn profile. With the completion of each Step, I could see and feel Emily's confidence returning. She began a great new career approximately 90 days after we began to work.

As a coach, I enjoy assisting my clients to discover the value of a LinkedIn profile that helps them reconnect with friends, former associates, and ultimately the power to introduce them to a connection for their new career!

Take a moment to reflect on the changes that technology has created in the workplace over the past 25 to 50 years. My industry, talent attraction, has gone through amazing change — from newspaper ads and typed paper resumes mailed through the U.S. Postal Service to today when your resume is created using word processing software and emailed immediately or submitted directly to a company online — no more need for Wite-Out (so old that spellcheck shows that brand name as an error!). Your industry has probably experienced the same amazing transformation. At our fingertips, we may access information that we could never easily access in the past.

With this new technology, we are hearing new terms: social media and social networking among them. Computers that used to fill whole air-conditioned rooms were not as powerful nor as fast as the ones we hold in our hands today. Consider that NASA utilized many female "human computers" using pencil and paper to send and return the United States Apollo astronauts to the moon. (With my math talent, that is inconceivable!)

This preface leads us to LinkedIn software that uses algorithms to suggest new connections and count how many searches for connections that we conduct. LinkedIn was originally developed to help professionals connect with each other. The founders may or may not have guessed how quickly professional recruiters would adopt LinkedIn as a new source of contact. When news got out that professional recruiters were searching for talent on LinkedIn, the numbers of professionals creating profiles on LinkedIn exploded. Currently, there are more than 467 million profiles on LinkedIn. Therefore, if you want to propel your career forward, using LinkedIn as a potential source to network is very powerful — you just need to know how to play. Teaching you is my job in Step 6.

> Recently, I was on a recruiting contract with HID Global, a cyber-security company. During a search for a Sales Channel Latin American sales professional, I identified a candidate with much of the right experience. She did not have a LinkedIn profile. The first question the Vice President of Enterprise Sales asked was, "Should I be concerned that she does not have a LinkedIn profile?"
>
> His question demonstrates the focus managers put on LinkedIn profiles — your profile needs to be complete with a summary, work history, and education. If you served on any volunteer boards or leadership/coaching for nonprofits, include that experience. The nonprofit may be a passion for that organization.

Let's talk about social networking. During the past few years, you have been bombarded with all kinds of social-networking opportunities — LinkedIn, Facebook, Twitter, YouTube, Instagram, Snapchat, Pinterest, etc. More are on the way. If you are not comfortable with iPhones, iPads, Android phones, Microsoft Surface pads, and other handheld computers that allow you to talk, check e-mail, and set appointments simultaneously, you probably are not very comfortable with the social media tools. On the other hand, maybe you're more "OMG U text 4 hrs!"; and know these tools are simply arrows in your quiver. You have guessed the power of Science in LinkedIn. Both Computer Science and Mathematics played roles in developing this powerful tool.

Since you most likely are nearing or over 50, LinkedIn is a powerful tool to embrace if you want to take charge of your career. Using LinkedIn in a larger company, you may be able to broaden your career within your own company by identifying managers in the new area that you would like to work. If you are a person already working at a high level within their company, those managers will be more interested in connecting and learning more about you. All managers like the easy hires where there is not the need to spend hours identifying and recruiting from the outside.

Many of you who are reading this book are simply looking for a new position outside of your current or recent past company. LinkedIn provides you with the opportunity to grow your connections in any way you like — industry, a field of work, location, title, and company.

> Several months ago, I spent an hour with a woman journalist with 40 years of experience in the newspaper business. She was recently laid off from a city newspaper in a massive layoff. Not interested in retiring, she was actively looking for a new position. We discussed who she should invite to connect and contact. Then I demonstrated how to search for those editors and publishers on LinkedIn. She was amazed at how powerful a tool was within her reach for free. For example, I found an editor who graduated from my college and was the editor of the newspaper in that city. I invited him to link with me, using our college mascot's name in my invitation. He accepted my invitation within 12 hours. She will grow her network nationwide using LinkedIn. She is a talented writer. Later, she chose to begin a freelance writing business and used her LinkedIn connections to attract new business.

Once you begin developing your brand as a candidate or employee, it's good to develop your profile on LinkedIn. Working on LinkedIn can take as much time as you want to dedicate to it. That is my caution to candidates and companies alike: Every networking/sourcing method costs something. Sometimes it's money; sometimes it is time. If it is time, it must be done well, or you (or they) lose credibility with your audience. Remember to work on your LinkedIn profile when you cannot network — early morning or in the evening — outside of prime networking time.

Most job seekers do not view themselves as marketing experts. While you do not need to be a marketing expert, it is important to follow basic marketing fundamentals:

1. Identify your market (companies where you would like to work).
2. Research what type of people they hire (and determine if you are one of those).
3. Create a brand that demonstrates the expertise the target companies are looking for and make sure that is reflected in your profile summary.
4. Use the same verbiage to describe your responsibilities and accomplishments in your profile that your target companies use to describe the same work (Remember speaking their language?).

5. Create short 400 to 600 word blog posts weekly or monthly that demonstrate your expertise and publish them on LinkedIn. Content is a powerful attraction!
6. Join industry groups on LinkedIn and share your blogs with those groups (if they meet the group standards).

Now you have a high-level view of branding your experience on LinkedIn. Let's dig into the details of performing these tasks. Remember, the little things that you do in your search that may make a big difference. Ever hear the adage, "The devil is in the details?"

## Developing Your LinkedIn Profile

When you are on LinkedIn on your home page, there is a horizontal menu on top. Look to the right on that menu and you will see "Me" (of course, meaning YOU!) with a drop-down menu. In the drop-down, click "View Profile." This is where you go to edit your profile.

Let's peek at your LinkedIn URL. Every person has their own URL on LinkedIn. When you create a profile on LinkedIn, it assigns you a general URL that you may customize. Your general URL is a combination of your name followed by 6 to 9 letters/numbers that assign you a profile page (it almost looks like comic strip cursing!). When you look at your profile on LinkedIn, look at the URL in the browser line (the www. line) to see your LinkedIn URL. Were you aware that you could customize it? For instance, my LinkedIn profile URL is https://www. linkedin.com/in/recruiterguy/. (Take this time to invite me to connect with you — in your invitation, tell me that you are reading my book).

This is an easy process. When you look at your LinkedIn profile, in the upper righthand corner of your profile is "edit public profile and URL." Click there and you see "Edit your custom URL." Click on the blue pencil image to edit. Then create your own personalized LinkedIn URL. It may be your name "johndoe" or a combination of name and numbers "marysmith2019" (use something other than a birthdate) or something that describes your brand like mine, recruiterguy. You may have to try several combinations before you find one that is not being used. Once successful, remember to SAVE!

> One of the women I coached used MaryJonesEconomist (pseudonym) as her URL. Mary Jones was probably taken in the first year of LinkedIn. This enabled Mary to brand herself in her LinkedIn URL.

While in this section, I suggest that you make your profile easy to find. Drop down to "Edit Visibility." Click on "Public" to have the largest number of people able to find your profile via LinkedIn, search engines, and other services. Then click all the buttons to "Show" so all those sources may find you.

Congratulations! You have a customized URL that creates the perception of being a creditable LinkedIn user and your profile is more easily found. The very easy work is complete! Now let's work on the meat of your profile — your photo, your title, summary, experience, education, and volunteer experience.

Do you have a professional headshot? According to LinkedIn and LinkedIn experts, a professional headshot will attract 10 to 20 times the number of profile views than a profile without a professional headshot. If you have a professional headshot, ensure it was not taken too long ago — not a good idea to surprise a recruiter or a hiring manager. They will see the different "you" when you interview. Once you load your headshot, remember to click SAVE. It is painful to begin a second time!

Complete the professional experience on your profile within two days because people will begin to search on it immediately. Before you begin to complete the text portions of your LinkedIn profile, I suggest creating each addition in Word, then copy and paste from your document. This allows you to catch typos. Remember to check for the common errors that are often found in resumes — Manger/Manager, Mange/Manage — and that make it through spell check.

Feel free to complete an area and Click SAVE. Then stop to reflect on your success so far. It is always good to celebrate all your successes — even the little ones!

Let's begin with your title. You may use either your job title or **a title that best describes you.** Remember you are creating a brand for everyone who views your profile. You may also create a tagline that describes what you do and then add your title. This is my title to use as an example — *Helping organizations Recruit, Onboard, Actuate, and Retain Top Talent...Speaker/Author/Career Coach/Recruiter.* A person viewing my profile instantly knows what I do. Try to keep your tag line to 9 words or less, plus your title. For instance, let's say you decide to buy a franchise or start another type of business. You may use that title on your profile. Your LinkedIn profile is important because most managers will look to see it before they call you — and if you are a consultant, I guarantee you they will search for your LinkedIn profile.

> Executives and employees at Latitude Communications, one of my clients in Silicon Valley, were passionate about triathlons. (Latitude Communications was formerly known for their product, MeetingPlace, a data/video teleconferencing product until they were purchased by Cisco.) The company supported a San Francisco Bay nonprofit that organized triathlons. Many of their employees competed, including the CEO. If you had "triathlete" on your profile, they felt you may be a good fit for the culture, if your skills and experience were also appropriate.

You could spend a weekend and focus on your profile. I realize it is not as much fun as golf, tennis, hiking, etc. but those only give you momentary pleasure. A strong LinkedIn profile could attract the right person to recruit you for a job you love. It is definitely worth your time.

Your summary (LinkedIn now calls it "About") is important because it gives viewers a longer snapshot of your brand and experience. Click the pencil in the top right corner of the About section to begin editing. In the first two lines, include your phone number and email address. You may delete them from About after you find a new position. Make it easy for recruiters and hiring managers to contact you. In the About section, you may discuss your professional passions. So few people are passionate about their professional lives, you will stand out! Discuss a summary of your experience, including any amazing accomplishments. Click SAVE!

Now you need to focus on the Experience section. That same blue pen is in the corner. Click on it to edit your experience. Then click the plus sign to add positions at companies. You may simply cut and paste the experience from your resume including the start and end date. Ensure your accomplishments are visible. As a best practice, click SAVE after you complete each position.

> Many times, candidates say "But I don't want to brag!" My response, "If you are ever going to brag, Now is the Time!" If what you say is the truth, you are not bragging. You are

> stating facts. Those facts help me, as a recruiter, determine
> if I want to recruit you.

By completing your professional experience while including your accomplishments with metrics, if you have them, you have created a brand for yourself. What does your brand tell readers? If you want to improve your brand on LinkedIn, determine first what you want your readers to believe about you and your experience. While tweaking your LinkedIn profile, introduce your tweaks to your resume. Remember, if your accomplishments are not on your resume nor your LinkedIn profile, generally they will not be mentioned during interviews. One small misstep like that could mean the difference between receiving an offer and finishing a close second place. Once you SAVE your tweaks and reread them, are you happy with the result? If not, no problem. Have a relative or professional associate read it and ask them for their suggestions. Sometimes the fresh eyes of someone who knows you can add immeasurable benefit. They may remind you of an important accomplishment that you downplayed.

**Congratulations! The majority of your work on your profile is now completed!** Still more to do but if you stopped here, a reader could have a sense of your background and brand.

Now let's focus on the next step (these will be easier and less time consuming). Your education is next for addition to your profile. Add your college and degree (if you earned a degree). Click SAVE. Since my high school, DeMatha Catholic High School in Maryland is known nationwide, I added it to my profile. You never know what may spark a conversation. If your high school is also well known, feel free to add it and click SAVE. Do you have any certifications — Lean, Agile, Scrum, CPA, CISSP, CSP, CPAE, etc.? Be sure to add them and add current if they are current. Click SAVE.

Next is Volunteer Experience. Remember what I said about triathletes at Latitude Communications? This is the area where you list your volunteer participation. Add any leadership responsibilities during your volunteer work and then click SAVE.

The next section is Skills and Endorsements. You may add your skills and receive endorsements from people who have worked with you in the past — and interestingly, some from people who only know you through your LinkedIn profile. As always, click SAVE.

People who have worked with you in the past may write recommendations for you based on their experience. You may accept or decline their recommendation. I tend to give more recommendations than I receive. That is fine. You may do the same. I never ask for a recommendation, but you may if you feel your experience with that person merits a recommendation. All this material on your profile helps recruiters and managers see your depth and breadth of experience.

Have you been quoted in a publication or newspaper? Have you been interviewed on television and have the video? Have you been interviewed for your expertise on a podcast? All these can be added in the next section, Accomplishments. Then add your links to Publications.

I know you are saying "Humbert, I just need a job — not write a book!" All this work will be paid back to you in multiples of the time expended. There is a little secret to my madness. When you look at your completed profile, do you feel a sense of accomplishment? You certainly should. You proved yet again that you can accomplish something you did not feel you could accomplish. If you have a strong profile already, congratulations! Make some small tweaks in it and move to the next challenge — strengthen your brand.

# Brand Building with LinkedIn Articles and Posts

Far too often, professionals complete their profiles without considering an important aspect of LinkedIn — engagement with your network that employs both the Sciences of Psychology and Sociology. This is part of *The Science of the Over 50 Job Search*. Now that your profile is complete, you are building your brand. Just having a profile is important. However, if you want to develop a perception of expertise in your area that continues to grow over time, it is important to take the next step.

In the top navigation bar, click on HOME. You will see the feed from members of your LinkedIn network. If you agree with their posts, click "Like." If their post truly resonates with you, you may comment on their post. Focus on people or companies that you are targeting. With that reply, you may be building the perception of expertise within your LinkedIn network. Remember, no negative posts! People will see them too.

If you see an article or video that is pertinent to your field or industry, you may share the link by clicking HOME on your menu on top. Click on share a post. Type a short note about why you feel this is important information for your LinkedIn network and add the link to the article or even YouTube video to your post. Thank everyone who comments on your posts — and possibly even engage with them.

Simple additions like these will help you improve your brand and demonstrate expertise. I suggest if you belong to a LinkedIn group, click on their page and share your post with them (quickly peruse their page to ensure no one else posted the same article or video recently).

# LinkedIn Groups

This is the perfect segue to LinkedIn Groups. Click on HOME at the top of the page. Below your photo, you will see the groups where you created a post recently. You may click on the name of the group to go directly to their site on LinkedIn. Below your recent groups are the list of all your groups where you are a member.

What do you do if you haven't joined any groups? Return to the menu at the top of LinkedIn. On the far right, you will see "Work" with a drop-down menu. Click on "Work" and you will see an icon for "Groups." When you click on "Groups" you will see a search box at the top of the page. For practice, type "Project Manager" in the search box. Then click on "Project Manager in Groups." Look at the list of Project Manager groups and pick the ones where you want to join. Most will show you their rules — generally, they want expertise not advertising. Some groups are "Open", and you may simply click "Join." Other groups are moderated, and you must click "Join" and wait for the moderator to accept you into the group.

Here is a RecruiterGuy method to improve your acceptance more quickly. When you click on a group, look at the right column and you see the Group Admins. Click on each of the Admins and invite them to link with you. When you write your invitation always write a note and mention that you recently requested to join their LinkedIn group. Remember to read the Group's rules. It is important to follow their rules — generally, they prohibit self-promotion. You may discuss topics that demonstrate expertise but be careful when it appears it is all about you — and not the members of the Group.

Once you have joined the Group, read some of the posts, particularly by the moderators. This practice helps you learn what are appropriate posts in the Group. Every Group is different. Ensure your posts are appropriate for that Group.

When you attend networking meetings, ask the organizer if they will allow time for people with smartphones to find other people in the meeting and invite them to join each other's network? Add the LinkedIn app. Then, click on the blue people+. Then click on search people around me. Everyone in the room who has the LinkedIn app open to this area will see you and may invite you — and you, them.

This will give you a nice foundation for your LinkedIn profile and your LinkedIn branding. **Congratulations! This was a time-consuming exercise. It did help you reinforce your brand — or better yet — create your brand!**

## What Is the LinkedIn Lunacy?

As an active recruiter on LinkedIn, there is an opportunity to view the lunacy almost daily. The lunacy is presented by professionals in their profiles, some with multiple typos. What do those typos say about their professionalism? If a professional does not care enough to complete their profile, why bother? The impression that person gives detracts from the perception of their professionalism.

Since I am a political party agnostic, it is interesting to me when so-called professionals use this forum to attack members of the opposite political party. This is truly LUNACY! What happens if the company you are targeting has hiring managers who are members of the other political party persuasion? I understand freedom of speech — and the freedom to hire people who are the proper cultural fit. Your choice.

If you want the benefit of placing your profile on LinkedIn, take the time to brand yourself as a professional.

## What About Other Social Media for My Search?

**Separate your social networking from your professional networking.** If you connect with a company on Facebook, that company may see your posts and pictures. Some may be embarrassing, or worse, disqualify you from a job.

> The owner of a recruiting firm told me they introduced a candidate to a financial institution. The interview went very well, so well they extended a contingent offer to the candidate. The candidate accepted their offer. The company is very thorough when they vet their candidates. The client looked up the candidate on Facebook. The person enabled everyone to see his pages. Evidently, some of his posts to friends were viewed to be unacceptable for this firm and they rescinded the offer. Remember, everything that is public may be viewed and used in the final decision to determine if you are the best fit for a position.

In today's world, there is sometimes a temptation to criticize companies and individuals while feeling there is anonymity. Unfortunately, with a little bit of sleuthing and some carelessness by the person creating the negative post, they may be identified. Once a person is identified as a negative poster, a social media trust is broken that may not be ever regained.

## Like it or not, you are constantly being measured by someone.

Take your LinkedIn profile seriously. Make it a dynamic profile by creating an interesting professional post or a short article on some aspect of your expertise. Try to post at least weekly. Once you land your favorite new position, continue to post regularly. I may be looking for you for my client ...

Remember your bookmark? This is a great place to use it if you need to work on your LinkedIn profile.

Creating or updating your LinkedIn profile adds more threads to your tapestry brand — and more self-confidence as you demonstrate your talents and accomplishments.

Completing this Step requires a little celebration! You have improved your visibility among professional recruiters and managers who are curious about you. Completing this Step better prepares you for your interviews because it freshens your memories of previous positions.

You are transitioning from creating the foundation of your Career Search to the action that ultimately will power your search. The last 6 steps provided with the threads of your tapestry branding — a professional picture of you, your skills, experience, and attributes have been created.

Consider how a completed and professional LinkedIn profile with comments and blogs strengthens the perception of your expertise. This continued practice builds upon the threads of your tapestry of skills, experience, and brand.

**In the spirit of visualization, every morning when you are preparing for your day, and every evening before bed, stand in front of the mirror. Look at yourself and smile confidently. Then say aloud . . .**

-------------------------------------

# I Am A Professional!
# I GOT THIS!

-------------------------------------

The practice of visualization is a powerful psychological tool. If you network faithfully, utilize LinkedIn, and practice visualization, you improve your chances of finding a job much sooner. Is it worth trying? What do you have to lose? Once you find your new position, continue to practice visualization in your work and personal lives.

-------------------------------------

*Now let's examine*

# STEP 7 —
# Successfully Sourcing Hidden Positions

-------------------------------------

**STEP 7**

# SUCCESSFULLY SOURCING HIDDEN POSITIONS

In November 2020, I coached a CFO who was disappointed to find there were only two CFO positions posted on the job boards he checked. Neither position was interesting to him because the companies were too small.

Successfully sourcing hidden positions requires curiosity and patience. We know those positions are out there, but how do we locate and identify them, especially when we are in a pandemic? It is important to understand that many companies intentionally do not post positions that are director level and above. Those positions are typically filled through networking with the top executives or placed with a retained executive search firm. Smart companies prefer candidates who are networked to them through trusted sources. These sources verify the validity of the candidate's skills, experience, and attributes — many as the result of working directly with them.

As a person with more than 25 years of experience in the professional work world, you experienced many situations where a manager suddenly pivoted and asked you to drop what you are currently doing and jump in a new direction. This is your experience right now. You reach for your bootstraps — and pull them up. Then you go in a new direction and accomplish the new expectations.

My experience as an executive career transition coach taught me that many executives and salaried employees have the same feelings as you. Understand that you are still experiencing the stages of grief that we discussed in Step 1. You are working towards acceptance and the best way to reach acceptance is to speak with other people about your successes.

Review the "Here I Am!" Step 3. This book is not a novel. Well, in a way it is. **You are learning to be the author of your new book that describes your steps to success.** There will be highs and lows, successes and failures during your search. Embrace your journey! You are on a path to benefit your career, your family, and indeed, your new company once you have identified it.

Treat this book as a reference to uncover the science of your career search. Return to Steps when you need to review them. When coaching professionals, oftentimes I need to return to the basics — previous steps to continually build towards the future. This is part of the science of a successful search, knowing when you need to review what you learned in the past. Understanding the science of your communications with your mind, and the importance of giving your mind positive thoughts is crucial at this point in your search.

Up until this point in your career, there may have been a few times when you started from the beginning in your search. For many professionals, through their career, they were approached by someone who worked with them in the past or were approached by recruiters who received their name and contact information from someone who knew them. Their search was handed to them on a platter. You may have had this same experience. For others — though this is not as common as it was in the past — you may have worked for the same company for your entire career.

> Last year, I worked with an accountant who went to work with a company as soon as he graduated from college. He worked hard and made many contributions to the improvement of the company's products. After 35 years of employment, his employer experienced a downturn and laid him off. You may imagine his despair. He had no clue where to start his search.

> We worked together. He learned how to conduct a proper job search. He experienced the highs and lows. After a period of persistent search, he first identified a company that needed his experience. Then he networked his way into that company. Today, he is happily employed — and has continued to network.

You will reach this success too. Not only is it important to learn the structure . . . successful search for a new position, but it is also important to learn the science of a successful job search. Let's do this!

Think like a detective — or a recruiter. Utilize that curiosity that you developed as a child. Everything was new for you then. "Why?" was one of your favorite questions to ask — over and over and over again! Your poor parents and teachers! This was how you learned. Dust off your talent for sourcing companies that need your expertise and people who may introduce you to those companies. You replace "Why?" with "WHO?"

You are acquiring knowledge. This is the foundation of successful sourcing. Who needs my services? How do I identify them? Who may introduce me to them? What skills are transferable to a new industry? How may I utilize this newly found industry knowledge to benefit my new employer? Interestingly, for this aspect of your search, you are utilizing Computer Science as a user.

The time you spend acquiring this new knowledge will reward you in unexpected ways. It is important to identify target companies and potential networking contacts. Your research will also benefit you during your interviews when you discuss your research and the surprising discoveries you made. Hiring managers generally like to hire candidates who demonstrate industry knowledge — even if they come from an unrelated industry. These skills are described as transferable skills.

## Where Can You Acquire New Knowledge?

The tools are virtually everywhere in today's world. Let's try the Internet first because it has a long reach. Both Microsoft's Bing and Google are a start. In our last step, we discussed LinkedIn as a source of information.

At this point, acquire knowledge. Don't simply focus on job listings. Well, take a quick peek but don't spend more than a few moments. Look for companies who need your service. Then research their websites. How has their market focus changed? Have they improved their products or services recently? Do they need someone with your talent to bring fresh ideas? Remember, there are skills that every company needs to function. Some of those skills are executive, finance/accounting, sales, marketing, operations, human resources, me (I mean, recruiting), etc. depending on their industry.

Click on the company's press releases. Are they promoting a new product or service? What is their news? If they do not have recent announcements, there is a need for a marketing professional with innovative press release experience . . . and many companies have that need.

If they are a public company, click on their quarterly earnings call. Learn how the market or even a pandemic is impacting their business. How may you help them?

After you research their website, go to LinkedIn. In the search box on LinkedIn, type the company's name. Click on the company when the results come up. Then click on "See all 2,359 employees on LinkedIn" to see the names of the people who work for the company on LinkedIn. Pick and choose who you want to link with on LinkedIn. Is this a great world — or what?

Who is on their board? Most times board members are listed with a short bio on a company website. You may have to search to find them. Begin with the "About Us" page on the site. If you are a senior executive, these are people you need to meet. They know and may be directing the CEO to attract a new executive member to their team. Typically, they also know board members from other companies because many times they sit on more than one board. Do you know any of the board members of the company you targeted? Did any graduate from your school? Are any board members neighbors? (You may have thought of them as Jane or Joe, without knowing what they did.)

An often-forgotten source is your local library, which is staffed with professionals who love helping community members acquire knowledge. Reference librarians don't simply look in books — what a novel idea! They know the best sources of information at any given moment. While at the library, read the local business journals and any available online archives of those journals.

There is another resource in the library reference section — the *MNI Manufacturers Directory*. They are printed by the state and list every single manufacturer in the state, even as small as one employee. The directory includes the name of the company, address, what they manufacture, their revenues, and executives' names. It can be a powerful tool. Remember, each of those companies requires sales, marketing, accounting, human resources, IT — the gamut of fields of work — not to mention skill positions within manufacturing.

Track the companies that you are researching. You may use Excel, Word, One Note, or — old school — a notebook. I recommend Excel because you may easily add rows or columns — and search on names in the list, but it doesn't matter how you track them. Leave space for new additions to your knowledge. This is an important task for several reasons, but most importantly, it grows your knowledge of your previous industry and may introduce you to a new industry that is crying for your skills.

> Many times, executives frustratingly asked me how to find a specific talent when we were discussing a talent attraction contract. We discussed their process and their current methods. Too often, their human resource departments focused only on posting positions to job boards and called that practice "recruiting" or "talent acquisition." When I asked if their recruiters were direct sourcing, they asked, "What is that?" I responded, "Networking with their hiring managers to identify potential candidates or people who might know potential candidates."
>
> One of those clients was Trex Company. When I met with the CEO, he asked me why companies pay me so well? I responded, "Think about your question for a moment. You flew me to Dulles Airport and rented a car for me to drive to Winchester, VA. I interviewed with your HR director, who decided I had the skills to recruit successfully for you. Then she asked me to interview with you. Trex Company paid for my meals and put me up in a nice hotel overnight. Now I am interviewing with you. You obviously are feeling pain in recruiting. My job is to make your recruiting pain go away." He hired me on the spot — and I did make their pain go away by recruiting top talent. Two years later, Trex Company invited me back a second time.

Conversations with members of your network may lead to consulting opportunities similar to the one I had with Trex Company. Aren't leaders in every company consulting and building consensus within their organization? Therefore, your consulting with your network connection may lead to a full-time career interview.

LinkedIn Groups have hundreds of groups across most industries. In the LinkedIn search box, type the industry name (for example, Manufacturing) and you will have three choices:

1. Manufacturing in Jobs
2. Manufacturing in People
3. Manufacturing in Groups

Click on Manufacturing in Groups. Join appropriate groups. Then read some of their discussions. The people in these discussions may be people you know through work, church, school, etc. The discussions will also give you an insider's knowledge of the industry — and companies who may need your skills. You may also see the list of the members of the group. Who do you know?

Don't sell yourself short — unless it is deserved. In some instances, people are released because they have not kept current with industry standards. If that is the case, search industry-related associations for certifications to earn to bring your knowledge up to date. In those certification classes are other people with similar interests who may be able to help you identify a new company you are not aware of.

Have you looked at the member companies of your local Chambers of Commerce? You may be surprised to find a company in your town or city that you did not know existed previously. Generally, they have a website to x-ray (probe for your benefit).

As mentioned previously, most companies do not post director-level or other executive-level positions online. There are many possible reasons why companies do not post those positions. Here are a few:

1. There is an incumbent and they do not want that person to hear the company seeks to replace him or her. For the recruiter, this is the definition of a "confidential search". You may have either been the beneficiary of such a search; or possibly the victim of one.
2. The company has a succession plan in place and knows who they will promote.
3. Some companies do not have the internal talent to source and screen high level professional candidates.

4. Companies may not want to be involved in directly sourcing candidates from other companies; and, prefer some plausible deniability. They don't want other companies to learn that they are poaching. I tell my clients they may reply that they told their contract recruiter to stay away from that company — Bad RecruiterGuy!

Have you checked with the local city/town economic development organization? They brag about the new companies they attracted to the area. How about the state economic development agency? When we decided to leave Iowa, I met with the Utah Governor's Office of Economic Development in Salt Lake City. They convinced me to bring my consulting business to Park City, UT.

# Find Companies Who Need You (Even If They Don't Realize It Yet)

Curiosity and building a foundation of knowledge are the key goals. Now is a time to understand something. This gathering of knowledge may become all-consuming. Remember proper goal setting using SCAMPS? This is an opportunity to use SCAMPS. Determine specifically how many companies you need to research. Create a strategy to gain knowledge. Make it challenging so your brain gets excited! Also, determine if your goal is attainable. Then set a specific end date. That date to today's date tells you how many companies you need to research per day — is it challenging enough or too challenging? Finally, make your goal public among the people who support you.

> Time for a personal point. It is important to discuss your plan with your family or significant other. They may want to assist you but have no idea how to do so. They will hold you accountable — and allow them to do so. Since I have been married for 48 years to an amazing wife, I can tell you what happens if your spouse feels you are not working hard enough on your job search. Your "Honey Do List" grows rapidly. Stay focused on your job search tasks.

Of course, go online. Try these job boards to identify potential target companies and openings — just don't apply yet:

- www.Indeed.com — now the largest job board
- www.Monster.com — lost some of its shimmer, but still a tool to be used.
- www.CareerBuilder.com — falling further behind Indeed
- This is a list of 50 niche job boards (niche job boards focus on specific, and sometimes, narrow fields of work, i.e., accountants, nuclear plant engineers, banking, etc.): https://www.smartrecruiters.com/blog/best-50-niche-job-boards/

The Financial Executive Networking Group (www.thefeng.org) learns about executive openings and shares them with its membership. This is primarily for CFO professionals and is described as a niche group. You will need to find a member who will sponsor you — and you may network directly with them.

This is your research to find companies and openings. You have created a list or a spreadsheet that lists companies who are or have searched for people with your skills. Your spreadsheet should include a column for the company's website.

**Importantly, this is how you identify companies who do not yet know they need you. Congratulations! Now that you know how to source hidden positions, you may practice searching while adding to your networking activity.**

## Experience Equals Networking Power

Does age discrimination occur? Not legally, but of course, it occurs. I have been a recruiter long enough to watch it bite some people who in their thirties claimed that people in their fifties would not understand the current market. Time flies by for all of us. Suddenly, they are in their fifties and out of work. They claim, "It is not fair! The younger generation says we are too old to understand the new generation." Love it when karma works! Please understand that the best action is to find someone in that company who has worked with you and knows how your skills will benefit that company. Then introduce you to a decision-maker. If you are unable to network your way in, the only effective action is to simply move on. At this point, you do not need the negative energy from pounding your head against a wall.

Remember, in large companies, the most junior person in human resources is the person retrieving resumes from the applicant tracking system. As I discussed in Step 4 unless the system identifies you as a perfect fit, you will not be chosen — and your resume will remain in the black hole.

Now that you know what percentage of positions are filled through networking, let's discuss the metrics the career transition industry discovered about professional jobseeker activity.

If you talk/meet with two new people per week, it will take you a year to find a job. If you talk/meet with 10 new people per week, it will take you six months to find a job. Sobering, huh?

**If you talk/meet with 20 new people per week or four per day — two in the morning and two in the afternoon, it will take you 90 days to find a job.** In my experience coaching executives, these numbers hold very true.

> Several years ago, a senior account executive with a successful 24-year IBM career followed by a successful career with another company was laid off during a reorganization. (Remember what I said about companies not doing a good job measuring employees' worth?) This person knew how to sell!
>
> She attended several of our May Park City Career Network meetings. Then she shared that she wanted to take the summer off to spend it with her children. Certainly understandable. At the end of August, she called and said she needed to get going on her search. We chatted about her required effort. She committed to finding a job in 90 days. This professional set about networking with at least four people per day. Almost to the 90 days later point, a top tier consulting organization hired her; and she is successfully selling on the enterprise level. She did it through networking persistently.

Celebrate your success in learning how to source the hidden positions! Practice searching the positions and finding people on LinkedIn — or even among your list who work at these companies. You may try the reverse, look up your friends from your list, using LinkedIn. Wouldn't be nice to discover they are now working at one of your target companies? Stranger things have happened! If you know executives who are members of boards of companies, network with them. They may be aware of a company that needs your talents and experience. NEVER assume anything negative! Always assume someone will assist you! All of this research builds confidence and bulks up your tapestry brand.

**You can do it! Now you know why you need at least 500 names. You will go through 80 contacts per month. The next chapter teaches you how to effectively network and keep building your list of contacts.**

# Job Search PROCESS Checklist

- Let's go to the beginning. Where do you feel you are relative to the stages of grief? Why do I keep bringing this up? I want you to be aware of your feelings — and know this is normal. Now add the visualization of suc-cess finding the perfect job! (Science of Psychology)
- This is very important: How many people are listed in your networking spreadsheet? It's important to get your number up to 500 or more names and contact numbers. Remember, you just need to know the name of the company. Look up their company's general phone num-ber — old school sourcing! Today, you generally do not need to worry about a receptionist screening you out. The automated answering system directs you to click on #3 to search the directory. Then type the first four letters of the person's last name. How easy!
- Are you still adding skills and attributes to your lists? You will occasionally remember something that you forgot. Remember to add them, aster-isk the ones that you enjoy, and build a story around the 4 W's — What was the challenge, your analysis and action, your result, and what you learned? You will need this for your interviews.
- Take time to review your LinkedIn profile. Ensure it reflects your brand. Write articles of 400 to 600 words to build the perception of you as an expert professional. While unemployed work to add one professional article per week. This is your job — build credibility and a following on LinkedIn. (Perception incorporates the science of psychology)
- Are you actively building your LinkedIn connections? The more direct

connections, the more people you may network with successfully. Feel free to request a link with me. https://www.linkedin.com/in/recruit-erguy/ I have over 7,100 direct connections — and growing daily. You must have at least 501 direct connections so people looking at your profile see you have 500+ connections. Right or wrong, this is one way recruiters measure a professional's credibility.

• When you attend networking meetings, ask the organizer if they will allow time for people with smartphones to find other people in the meeting and invite them to join each other's network? Add the LinkedIn app. Then, click on the blue people+. Then click on search people around me. Everyone in the room who has the LinkedIn app open to this area will see you and may invite you — and you, them (sciences of sociology and technology).

• Check your LinkedIn privacy to ensure your connections may see professionals in your network. Otherwise, they may check after they accept your invitation and then remove you. That is my practice. You may select your privacy by clicking your photo in the top menu bar.

• (Science of Psychology) Tonight — and every night, stand in front of the mirror. Look at yourself confidently, smile, and say aloud:

------------------------------------

*I Am A Professional!*
*I GOT THIS!*

*Now let's prepare*
*to* **NETWORK**
*to a New Position*
*in* **STEP 8***!*

------------------------------------

# EXPECT SUCCESS!

# *NEWLY NETWORKING?*

Adrienne is a successful marketing executive. Her network, as you may imagine, was huge. She was not shy — until it came to networking for a new position. She did not want to impose on her friends, acquaintances, and business associates when her company folded.

When we met, we discussed where she felt her career should head. She was comfortable in the consumer marketing field and enjoyed working with product development and marketing. I asked her how comfortable she was networking with people she knew. She looked at me like I was crazy. We explored her thoughts. She simply was afraid to pick up the phone (Join the 10,000 pound phone club!).

We discussed the value of her Here I AM! speech. Then I positioned networking as a marketing exercise. Now she was a little more comfortable networking — at least try making a couple of calls. Fortunately, both calls were fruitful and she enjoyed her conversations with former business associates. After that, Adrienne was more comfortable picking up the phone and calling people in her network. Within a week

93

> or two, she had interviews set. Ultimately, she found an exec-
> utive position in a company you would know through her
> networking efforts.

The statistics mentioned at the end of the last Step bear repeating for emphasis on the importance of proper networking.

Over the past 45 years, the career transition industry (companies who are called upon to assist laid-off staff find their next position) tracked how people find their new jobs. Pay attention to these statistics — and remember, I'm a professional recruiter telling you this.

**In great economies or poor economies, 74% to 76% of all jobs are filled through networking.** Some human resource departments will tell you those numbers are wrong. They say that the resumes came from their applicant tracking system. They do not ask how the resumes found their way into the applicant tracking system. Generally, the candidate speaks with an employee within the company (networking) who tells them that the practice is to apply online. Then let them know your resume is in the system. They pull the resume and hand carry it to the hiring manager and endorse the person who is a friend, former coworker, or someone who was introduced to them through your network. Some companies reward this behavior by giving that person a referral bonus.

If 74% to 76% of all jobs are filled by networking, how many jobs are filled by applying online? For the past 10 years, approximately 8% of all jobs are filled by people applying online. Far too many professionals try to find a job the *easy way*. Get on Indeed/Monster/CareerBuilder and reply to job postings. How many positions are filled by professional recruiters like me? For the past 10 years, approximately 8%. The balance is filled through career fairs (speed networking, newspaper ads, families, etc.).

> One professional proudly told me he had applied to more than
> 200 positions on Indeed in the past month. When I asked him
> "How is that working for you?" His smile turned to a frown
> when he informed me that he had one interview — and that
> was for a position below his skill level.

Listen to the ads for Indeed. They brag about being the largest job board (they are). Then they advertise to the employers that they can screen for candidates who demonstrate they have the right skills for the job — great marketing! Translated, it means this enables the companies **to screen you out**. Interestingly shortly after Monster advertised they would screen candidates for companies, the candidates stopped posting their resumes on Monster. Recruiters saw fewer qualified candidates and companies began to leave Monster in droves. The same may happen to Indeed.

## How Does Science Impact Networking?

Many coaching clients are surprised when I mention the Science of Networking. They ask, "What does Science have to do with calling people?" The Science of Psychology teams with Computer Science in today's networking world.

When you create your networking list, what tools do you use? Some are old school — high school and college yearbooks, class lists provided by your schools, your holiday card list, family, close friends, neighbors, former coworkers, etc. Other tools utilize Computer Science — LinkedIn, Google, Bing, Facebook, Instagram, etc.

When you call members of your network, which Science kicks in? The Science of Psychology. Understanding people's motivations are the Science of Psychology. This Science is utilized throughout all of your networking. For instance, if you tell me that a mutual friend recommended that you call me to assist you in your career search, am I motivated to assist you? Absolutely! I do not want to let my friend — nor you — down. I also use the Science of Psychology when I recruit candidates and network with them to identify new candidates.

Everyone unknowingly uses the Science of Psychology daily. We do not think of it in those terms. We learned the Science of Psychology from our experience unless we received additional training in college or our employment. Some of our intuition is researched. We learned that some of our thoughts and feelings about others are ingrained into our minds, similar to fight or flee.

Isn't it nice to know that networking is a natural human action?

# A 3D Look at Business Interviews and the Importance of Networking

While writing this Step, I briefly chatted with business professionals to give you a three-dimensional sense how important networking was to their business — and how important it will be for YOU!

## 1. *The Professional Perspective*

### Vic Method, director, business development at Fall Line Capital

*Vic is a highly successful business development professional. He was kind enough to walk me through every job change in his career since 1981. Of 14 job changes, how many does he feel were though networking? Thirteen were made through networking! The one job change that was not found through networking did not end well. What lesson did Vic learn? Networking is the most effective way to find a new position.*

## 2. *The CEO Perspective*

### Mark Capone, former CEO of Myriad Genetics

*Mark said hiring appropriate talent is one of the hardest things to assess in business — interviewing, references, the role they play, drill down deep. In his experience, the most difficult aspect is the cultural fit. Some people are successful in their current culture but may not succeed in our different culture. Mark said his company may eliminate the danger of a poor fit if the candidate came in through a network he and his employees trusted. "Networking is the key to finding the best qualified candidate for your culture."*

*Mark and his staff went through extensive interviews with one candidate introduced by a trusted networking source; and decided they wanted to explore other candidates. They hired a retained recruiting firm to vet candidates for that position. After months of interviewing, they selected the candidate who was introduced by the trusted source. In Mark's experience The higher the level of the position, the greater the danger to the company if they are a poor fit.*

### 3. *Management Consulting Contract Perspective*

*Joe Patten, founder and CEO of MainStream Management, LLC*

*Joe founded MainStream Management LLC in 1998. When asked how many of his contracts were found by networking, his response was, "of the 200 or so contracts we have had between 1998 to 2020, only two were not found through networking."*

*His message to job seekers:*

> "When networking, a person must have persistence, passion, and a product the person or company wants to purchase." For job seekers, you are the product/service. Do whatever is necessary to determine the company's problem. Then be passionate about your ability to help them.

*Joe also said that one of the toughest skills for most people is to ask someone to introduce you.*

As you may see from Mark Capone's response above, this is how smart CEOs prefer to meet candidates, not someone who applies online. Make a game of it. Joe Patten's comments on the persistence, passion, and product/service for the potential apply to the message you present during networking. Make over 1,000 contacts per year (average four per day). Use your research to become a consultant. Ask more questions than they ask. Be passionate in your responses. If you are passionate as you help them, you will gain their trust — and quite possibly be hired.

### 4. *Independent Consultant Contract Perspective*

*Kathy Loveless, MS, CSP, founder and CEO of Loveless Enterprises, Inc.*

*Kathy is a member of the Million Dollar Speaker Club with the National Speakers Association. When asked what percentage of her speaking contracts over 50 years came from networking, Kathy replied that more than 98% of her contracts were found through networking. "This is a testimony of how much we trust our friends."*

## 5. RecruiterGuy.com Perspective

*Bill Humbert, CEO RecruiterGuy.com (Provocative Thinking Consulting, Inc.)*

*This is my business. Since 1992, 27 of my recruiting consulting contracts came to me through networking; and, only three came through other sources, including an attendee from a webinar where I presented.*

If you are serious about finding a new, exciting position, the evidence shows that networking is the best method to accomplish this goal.

# Network to Success Approach

Some professionals hesitate to use their network for their job search. Typically, they tell me the reason is an embarrassment, or the desire not to bother members of their network. Other times, they tell me their children are sick or they must babysit. When I ask them, "What do you do when you are working?" Their expression gives them away. It is an excuse.

> Recently, I was coaching a talented individual who is actively engaged in his search. Several times over a month, he told me that his child was ill, and he could not network because he had to take care of them. Other times, he told me that he had to babysit. Finally, I called him on his excuse. I told him, "It's not fair to your child that you are using him as an excuse to avoid networking. Use him as your reason to network!" He accepted my coaching and for the past two months has been networking with four new contacts daily — and enjoying networking success!

Many of you remember the mantra, **"It's not what you know, it's who you know!"** In today's world, it has been shortened to **"network to success"**. They both bring the same results. Network your way to finding a new position or even solving a problem in your current position.

Over the years, many people complained to me that they don't know how to network. I tell them they are being silly. All of us began networking when we were 4 years old, and asked, *"Where'd you get DAT?"* We continue to network when we asked, *"Who is an easy Professor of English?"* or *"Do you know a good mechanic?"* or *"What is your recipe for that delicious entree?"* Generally, we are not shy about asking those other questions. Literally, we have networked all our lives, just maybe not for a new career. Understand that most people have good hearts and want to help other people. That means you! Have you heard the slightly overused expression "paying it forward"? By assisting you in your search, they are paying it forward.

As a rookie recruiter, I was required to speak to 40 candidates per day. It was great training. I did not have the Internet in 1981. Heck, we did not have a computer! That came five years later. You can talk with four people per day. You got this!

## Connect Your Passion to Your Career

Many times, well-meaning people have asked me, "You have been recruiting since 1981. Why are you STILL just a recruiter?" My response is, "Where else may I help companies improve their profitability by identifying and recruiting the best candidate to propel their business forward? And, where else may I make impacts in people's lives by recruiting a talented individual who may be stymied in their current position to a new company and position where their career may blossom?" The reason I am still working and writing books to help people find jobs, companies find people, and both to properly set goals to become more successful is my passion to help people succeed.

What is YOUR passion? Are you passionate about your work — or are you just looking for a job? Far too many people are simply looking for a job.

> My dad was a person who was a very talented government auditor for the General Accounting Office. After he passed away only three years into retirement, I found out he despised every day that he worked. Sadly, he had a family to support and a job that he could not stand. He felt trapped with golden handcuffs — and did not look for another position where he would be happy. This situation potentially shortened his life.

Don't allow yourself to fall into his trap. The reason for your current search may be the universe allowing you to find a new position where you may make positive, measurable impacts and have fun! Find a position where you will enjoy your work, the people with whom you work, and a company that matches your values. Easy? Of course not, but is it worthwhile? Absolutely!

Once you decide on a new line of work that you love, possibly even in your current industry, your newfound passion will encourage you to network with as many people as you can to find the perfect position.

**If you have four or more conversations in a day, celebrate your success by doing something you enjoy. Reward yourself!**

**We've discussed WHY we network. Now let's discuss the HOW to network!**

One very important concept of networking is that successful networking involves both give and take. **The first step in successful networking is listening.**

Focus on the person who is speaking with you. What is the problem they are trying to solve? How may you help them? Ask them questions to help you clarify your thinking. Sometimes, it gives them a different perspective. Sometimes your perspective is all they need. Remember, if you build the reputation of being a problem solver as a networking partner, people will hear about you and your kindness. When it is your turn to reach out, they will be more welcoming and excited to hear from you.

You have years of experience that will benefit many people and companies. Your thoughts are important. Remember the law of nature — what you give is what you will receive. Look deep into your past. Have you received what you gave?

> I was a volunteer 7th and 8th grade girls basketball coach for over twenty years in Maryland and Iowa. My passion was to help my players improve, understand the game, appreciate basketball, and learn to be better teammates. Most importantly, I wanted each to believe in their contribution to the team. Two of my players invited me to their weddings. What an honor to celebrate with them! The more recent player took me aside as we were leaving her wedding reception. She said, "You were the first person to tell me my skills are valuable." You may imagine the tears that welled up from deep inside. She became a high school state track star and college track star. What you give is what you will receive.

Over your years of experience have you become known as a giving person? A mentor? If so, many people will want to assist you in your networking to a new position, more than you may imagine.

If you do not have that reputation, it is not too late to create it by becoming interested in helping other professionals. Simple things work. Have you run across a position that was not a fit for you, but you know it would be a great fit for someone else who is looking? Call them and let them know about the position — and who to call. That word will get out.

This could be a time for you to meet people in public once the six feet of separation Covid-19 guidelines are lifted. Go to a chamber of commerce after hours or networking social where you may meet new people from your community, mostly small business owners.

Be careful you do not become an opera singer warming up — Me, Me, Me, MEEEE! The person who is only interested in his or her own benefit. When I attend an after-hours event, I generally sit back and survey the crowd for the first 15 minutes. Opera singers are flitting about. I make note of who they are. Then I go about meeting the people they just gave their business card to — and listen to who they are trying to attract to their business. Sometimes I can make suggestions based on our conversations. Remember, it is always best to speak in terms of the other person's interests.

## What Steps Help You Network To A New Position?

The first Step is preparation. Remember what Joe Patten said in his interview with me about the importance of networking in his consulting business? Using your research, become a consultant for companies. It is a best practice to provide potential solutions to companies. I ask questions about company recruiting challenges and how they are trying to solve them daily. Then I provide them with potential solutions. Whether they utilize my services initially or not, they remember I gave them the solution. They will return for paid consulting.

Then prepare your "Here I Am" speech for your approach to them. This is also known as the one-minute commercial or elevator speech. In Step 3, we discussed how to create your "Here I Am" speech and gave you an example of the speech by the avionics engineer. Remember feeling his passion why he wanted to continue his career as an avionics engineer: "To make flying safer for the pilots and the people they fly . . ." It is important for you to feel that passion for what you do. You may have to reach back many years to retrieve your passion for your job . . . or is it time to find something totally new that you will enjoy doing and put your energy into becoming more successful?

How many of the 500 names, companies they work for, phone numbers, and sources have you compiled? Now is the time to pull out your spreadsheet and get serious about adding names to your list, even if you have 500 names. Take everything that you learned in the LinkedIn Literacy Step and source people who may know the people you need to consult to find your next job.

During your search for a new job, your most important commodity is names and phone numbers, especially referred names and phone numbers! The Science of Psychology enters here again. Far too often, career seekers have a short list of networking names to call. Then they panic with every call because they need to find a job. The stress becomes overburdening. The way to solve that challenge is to create a large list of contacts. Then, any single call is not stressful to create positive results.

Do you belong to any service organizations? Many people in our world cannot take time for those activities because of our work. However, this may now be a great way to meet community members, contribute to your community, and network. In Park City, UT, the Rotary Club is very active with both a morning club and a noon club. They are community focused organizations. When we lived in north central Maryland, the Lion's Club was very active. All these organizations are worthwhile for the community and you. Use your experience and skills to get out and benefit your community. Your generosity always returns to you from somewhere, may not be the people you helped. It may come from somewhere totally unexpected.

> Do you belong to Toastmasters? One woman I coached joined Toastmasters to improve her public speaking for her marketing career. One morning, she spoke passionately for seven minutes about an aspect of marketing. There was a manager from Deloitte in the audience who was so impressed he invited her for an interview. She was hired at Deloitte. You never know where those darn hiring managers may show up! The people you meet who match your passions may be able to help you find a company whose culture matches your heart.

# Your Second Networking Spreadsheet

Develop a second spreadsheet of companies you have targeted. Your list may be long (any company that may need an experienced accountant) or your list may be very targeted to a few companies (organizations in technology or research). Your list needs to be in front of you all day, every day as you network to find a person to introduce you to a hiring manager.

Spend time researching your targeted companies. Go to your library and ask if they have a copy of the D&B Hoovers database of people who work in the company. Then compare that list to your LinkedIn contacts. You may have more people to link as you compare the lists.

Once you have identified potential target companies, spend some time researching them. Comb through their websites. Where are the opportunities for you to help them? Try to understand their challenges. Who is their competition? Based on their websites, what challenges can you help them overcome? What questions are you prepared to ask during your interviews? This information is important while networking and during an interview. During your research, take copious notes — either cut and paste your notes on the company to a document or print pages of its website. Once you have researched on their website, Google, Bing, and Glassdoor, look at the company on LinkedIn. Then click on their people. See who you are directly connected, and who may be willing to link with you. You know how you learn best. During your research, you may discover the company is not a good fit for you. That's fine. It is as important for you to cross companies off your list as add them. Their competition may be the right company.

# Knowledge is Power!

### Practice, Practice, Practice

Several months ago, I coached an executive whose company was sold. As so often happens, the acquiring company took advantage of the "synergies" to rid themselves of extra staff throughout the organization. Far too often, acquiring companies make judgments on the "devil they know," a current grade B employee over an acquired new member of staff. This is the way top performers get caught up in layoffs.

This executive had a company at the top of his target companies list. Fortunately, he was able to network for an interview. While there, he discovered their culture was different than he expected — and not acceptable to him. He was very disappointed because prior to his interview, he was sure he wanted to work there.

Later, he found another company whose culture was a perfect match — and he networked his way to an interview where he was introduced to the CEO. Remember Mark Capone's remarks on the value of networking? It is almost scary how well it works . . . if you work it.

You are going through the same process right now. Some companies are added to your list. Others are crossed off. That is part of the process. Remember, you are trying to find that job that is so much fun you'll say, "Wow! I even get paid to do this!"

In a serious job search, you need to faithfully call at least four new contacts per day for three months. Exceed expectations and call more people in your network per day.

If you do, the law of averages will work in your favor and you will most likely receive interviews and an acceptable offer in 90 days. Now you know why names and phone numbers are your most important commodities. Do the math. If you do not faithfully call those numbers, it will take you longer to find a job — unless you are very lucky.

In March 2020, a director-level candidate I coached was seriously networking. He called four or more contacts daily for two months. During the Covid-19 Stay Safe, Stay Home pandemic, he was interviewed through video conferences with the executives of two companies. He received two offers within an hour of each other. He accepted an offer from his top choice company that offered him a vice president-level position — and started the following Monday!

There are two important lessons here:

1. Companies are always hiring, no matter the economy, and in this case, the pandemic.
2. Networking is worth the toil to find a new position!

Now it is time to clarify one small and very important piece of information. Note that I said call, not e-mail. Companies are doing much better protecting their networks from outside attacks and spam e-mails. Your contact may not receive your e-mail. On the other hand, they may see that you sent an e-mail but are so busy they didn't have time to respond immediately — and it was buried in their mass of email. I have been that person. Wasn't the road to hell paved with good intentions? There is another very important component of electronic communications. Texts and emails strip out the emotion and tone from the sender. Then you are dependent on the receiver to receive the same message in your tone and emotion. How often does that happen? Maybe 50% of the time. Call when networking so the receiving person may hear your voice and build a relationship with you.

Practice networking by calling family and friends who know you well. Tell them you need some practice networking. Then practice your Here I Am! Speech. Ask them if they have any suggestions. Everyone has opinions. Not only will they be happy to help, they will be excited you asked for their assistance. Feel free to script your Here I Am! speech. Read it in a conversational tone. If you create a Here I Am! Speech that speaks to your passion, you will remember it quickly. When you finish your Here I Am! Speech, ask your friends and relatives "Who do you feel I should speak with next? After they give you one or two names ask, "Would you please introduce them to me?" Practice your ask, Every. Single. Time!

Your resume and LinkedIn profile must be ready at this point because you are going public now! Managers will look at LinkedIn and ask you for your resume. All these Steps are intertwined. You may already have noticed. Impassioned Interviewing is next!

## It Is Go Time for Networking

Now that you have practice, it is time to make those first calls to contacts who may not be as close to you as your practice contacts. If someone introduced you to your new contact, look them up on LinkedIn first. You may find that you worked at the same company in your past, perhaps they have the same volunteer interests, or possibly even the same high school or college. Do a little research so you are more comfortable speaking with them.

You may say, "Our mutual associate (or friend), (name) suggested that you would be a helpful person for me to contact. Is this a good time to chat for 15 minutes — or would this evening be preferable?" They may prefer the evening because they are in the middle of a deadline now. Ask for the best number and time to call.

When you call back, ask if this time still works for them for 15 minutes of their time? Then say, "When I spoke with (name), he/she strongly suggested that I call you. I am networking my way to a new job and they recommended a conversation with you. May I tell you a little about my experience and what I would like to do next?" Then, give them your Here I Am! Speech. Discuss their recommendations with them. Remember, this is how you find hidden jobs. Then ask if they would introduce their recommended contacts to you?

Many career seekers ask their contact, "Do you have any jobs?" I guarantee that if you just ask them if they have an opening at their company, their kneejerk response 98 percent of the time will be "No." If the answer is no, you are done. Think of fishing. Sometimes, you are simply trolling to see if the fish will take the bait. When they do, you set the hook. This is virtually the same. You are telling them about your background — and then, ask "Who do you feel I should speak with next?" If they reply, "Are you speaking (or interviewing) with us?" Set the hook (just like fishing) and ask, "no, will you introduce me to the hiring manager?"

If they do not give you my favorite response, try to get at least four or five people's names and numbers from each person you call. These are your warm referrals. They may say they don't know anyone. Then ask, "Whom do you know at ABC company?" or, "Do you know anyone who lives in New England (or anywhere)?" Asking the latter question may help you get to a different part of the country without knowing anyone there yourself.

Remember six degrees of separation — by conducting six directed conversations, you may reach anyone in the United States. In some states or industries, there are only two degrees of separation.

What is a "warm referral?" When someone calls you and says that a friend or business acquaintance gave them your name and number, you are more open to receiving the call, right? Not only that, you do not want to disappoint your friend, so you try to help that caller. That's why you should seek warm referrals. A person you call out of the blue may not even take your call. If they do take your call, they may not be as likely to help you. (You still should make cold calls because they can lead to more warm referrals.)

Many times, someone I respected asked me to meet with a person who was out of work. I set aside some time and met with them. Why? I wanted to maintain the respect of my contact; and, meet or exceed their expectations. Remember to give back when you have the opportunity.

> In the early 2000s, an executive who was laid off from a manufacturing company came to me for coaching. I did not charge him for my coaching nor my time. We covered almost everything in this book, including salary negotiation. Within a relatively short time, he was hired by another manufacturing company. Several weeks after he started, my network informed me that he had 10 openings to fill. The next Monday morning, I called and left him a nice message. Since I recognized that he was probably busy, I waited another week and left a message. No reply. The following week I left my final message. No response.
>
> Two years later, he still had not replied. Then, out of the blue, he called me. He told me that he had been laid off again and wondered if I would help him again. When I asked him why he never returned my calls after he started his last job, his reply was, "I was too busy." My response, "Oh, I understand . . . I am too busy to help you again."
>
> You know how you would feel in the same position. Treat people as you prefer to be treated.

## Maximize the Value of Networking Meetings

So, we have discussed many elements of networking but haven't discussed networking meetings. They are another way for you to meet people. As one of the organizers of the Park City Career Network, I can say we encouraged members to help each other. In many large cities and some smaller cities, there are groups helping people searching for their next positions. I have spoken to such groups in Salt Lake City, UT; Park City, UT; Iowa City, IA; Cedar Rapids, IA; and Fort Collins, CO. If members hear of opportunities that may be best for another member, they refer them. As a member of the National Speakers Association, it is our practice to recommend a better speaker if someone asks if we may speak on a topic outside of our sphere of knowledge.

Many other organizations promote networking among the members. Your local chamber of commerce may offer "after-hours" meetings. Chamber members are generally given free admission and members of the community may join the "after hours" for a small admission price. In my experience, these meetings have cliques and few people are truly interested in networking. But people are only as interested in you as you are in them. You have the time. Use it to meet new people. Imagine the little RecruiterGuy.com on your shoulder encouraging you to meet just one more person. He or she may be a person that you can help. Then they are more open to helping you.

> Several years ago, I attended a conference. One of the presentations was by a noted author whose presentation was networking. During his presentation, he mentioned that when you are participating in networking meetings, totally focus on the person you're talking with. Obviously, if you are looking around the room while chatting with them, they know you really are not interested in their conversation.
>
> After the presentation, I went up to thank him for his information. Ironically, as we were chatting, he was looking around the room. He lost a lot of credibility that day. His point was spot on.

The person in front of you is the most important person in your world . . . at this moment. Treat people with respect. If you can make suggestions to help them, do so. If not, nicely excuse yourself and either leave or meet someone else. While "working a room," work very hard to maintain eye contact with the one person or group of people in your conversation. Do not look for your next conversation. Remember to pay attention. Sometimes a person will say something that triggers the right question from you and leads you somewhere totally unexpected — and worthwhile.

I mentioned that I coached 7th and 8th grade girls basketball. During our practices, I demonstrated running down the sideline looking at the ball handler with my outside arm and hand leading, mouthing I'm open for your pass! As an experienced professional, you also need to demonstrate that you are open to a conversation. Be prepared for unexpected opportunities!

# The Role of Recruiters

In the 1980s when I was a contingent (fee-based) recruiter in Washington, D.C., one of my best clients was The Washington Post's IT organization. In those days, The Washington Post had an excellent IT department, one of the best in the area. We had a great relationship. They knew that my referrals were right on target. One day I was downtown, meeting with the IT director at The Washington Post regarding some of his open positions. He even gave me a tour of the printing facilities that were at that time located in the same building. After the meeting, I stopped at a nearby restaurant for lunch. After I was seated, I began to let my mind and ears wander. Eventually, a conversation at the next table caught my attention. The woman was an IT professional (in those days we called them data processing), and she was being interviewed by a recruiter. As their conversation proceeded, I decided that she would be a great fit for The Washington Post. She had the perfect experience and attitude to succeed there. Since Katharine Graham was the publisher at The Post, there was no glass ceiling.

I decided that I was going to meet that candidate. Fortunately for me, my vigilance was rewarded. The other recruiter got up from the table, leaving her sitting there by herself.

Given the opportunity, I leaned over, apologized for listening in on her conversation, and asked if she would be interested in working for The Washington Post. She said, "Sure!" I asked her if she had an additional resume. She replied "No."

Then I asked her if she was available to interview the next morning at The Post. She replied that she was. I told her to fax her resume to me (no e-mail in those days) and to expect an interview at The Post at 9 AM the next morning. She agreed.

I called the IT director and told him that he "had an interview tomorrow morning at 9 AM." He laughed and asked if I had a resume. I told him not yet and told him how I met the candidate. He laughed again. I assured him that I would get the resume later in the afternoon.

When she faxed her resume to me, I forwarded it to the manager at The Post. He called me back right away. He said that he liked her background and would set everything up. When I called her back to set up the interview, I was so confident that she would receive an offer, I told her to expect an offer by 11 AM. (Today, I may not be so over-confident!)

At 10:30 AM the next morning, the director called me and was laughing. He said that he was going to extend her an offer. He had a problem — all three managers who interviewed her wanted her on their teams — and another manager was interviewing her right then. They were going to have to decide which team she would join. That was the moment that I let him know my little secret — I told her that she would receive an offer from him by 11 AM. We discussed what it would take money wise. He laughed again and said, "no pressure!"

At 11:05 AM, he called me again to say that he extended the offer to her at 10:50 AM — and she accepted at 10:55 AM. She left the building at 11 AM and was very happy.

The candidate called me about 11:15, right after leaving The Post. She was also laughing. She said her last interview was over at 10:50 AM. The manager met with her and just before 11 AM., he extended her an offer and she accepted. She asked how I knew. I replied that I knew my client that well.

A postscript to that story is that the other recruiter found out that she accepted the job at The Washington Post a couple of weeks later. He was very upset when she told him how we met, even wanted me to pay for lunch! He probably never left a candidate alone in a restaurant again after our incident. Neither did I!

Bottom line — prospects for networking surround you, and you never know when one will strike up a conversation with you. Be prepared to accept and engage in that conversation. Also, I did NOT have her resume when I set the interview. Networking can be that powerful!

Many people have asked me, "What about professional recruiters? What is their role?" You may expect as a professional recruiter, I would trumpet our role in your job search. We have an interesting problem when attempting to assist a person who is out of work. Most companies in today's world do not want to pay a fee for someone out of work. They feel they should be able to find them through their website postings. In my speech, "Make Your Company ROAR (Recruit, Onboard, Actuate, and Retain) Top Talent!," I point to the floor and ask, "Do You HEAR That?" It's people in the applicant tracking system screaming, 'Pick me. Pick ME!'" as I begin to jump up and down. "But no one knows how to get them out!" Sadly, in many companies, that is true.

On one of my recruiting contracts, the HR manager was so afraid I would find candidates they overlooked, that she required me to take HIPPA training before giving me access to the company applicant tracking system. I nicely mentioned that the applicant tracking system had no one's medical records. She said it was policy. I took their online HIPPA training and passed She never granted me access to the company applicant tracking system. The vice president sadly shook his head and said, "That's why we had to hire you . . ."

The time to develop relationships with good professional recruiters is while you are productively working. Give them your Here I Am! Speech minus "Who do you feel I should speak with next?" If they know someone, trust me, they will tell you.

Accept their calls warmly. If it seems they are calling too often, simply ask them to spread out the time between calls. Time is money to recruiters, and they should accept your request gracefully. If they do find an interesting opportunity, feel free to explore it. If it is the right opportunity for you, you may find yourself in an exciting new position. This is an example of taking control of your career.

Many times, I developed professional relationships with candidates without being aware of any positions that would interest them at the time. I just wanted to get to know them, their interests, their skills, and personality. We would talk as they made impacts in their current position. We often discussed their excitement about something that went very well and the frustration when things weren't going well. Many times, a year or two passed before the perfect position became available. When I called them, we already had a relationship and the process proceeded smoothly to their next position. Rarely does this process happen quickly, but the example at *The Washington Post* I told above demonstrates how unexpectedly and quickly it can happen.

Also understand a professional recruiter's responsibility is to the client. Clients pay recruiters to find the best possible match for them. Recruiters are not paid by the candidate. I wish I had a dollar for every time I've heard from a candidate that one recruiter or another "didn't do anything for me." Usually, I nicely say that it's not the recruiter's job to do something for them, but one will probably be happy to make some suggestions for their search.

## A Day at the Fair

Another potential source of networking is career fairs. I know some candidates refer to them as "cattle calls" and other not-so-nice names. But a career fair is a great place to meet people who work for companies that you may target, and to help you identify others that you did not know were in the area. I have spoken at more than 70 career fairs nationwide and worked a couple of hundred career fairs representing clients.

A skilled candidate may work a career fair as well as a teenager working the rides at Walt Disney World. Before the day of the career fair, look to see which employers plan to attend. Then go to their websites to research their open positions and any interesting press releases. Polish up your "Here I Am! Speech targeting that company. They may not have open positions posted, but they may have announced an expansion — the job postings just haven't appeared yet. The fair organizers will usually post a map showing where the different companies will be located. Understand that they don't always show up where they are supposed to, but generally, they will be where you expect.

On the day of the career fair, print 10 more resumes than you expect to need. Do not fold your resumes. Bring them in a portfolio where you can also take notes.

When you arrive at a career fair, the event organizers usually will ask you to register before entering. Sometimes they allow you to register electronically and use a memory stick to load your resume into their system. Many times, they forward all resumes to the companies that participate in the fair.

Now, I am going to give you the secret to working at a career fair. It is one that every teenager knows when "working" an amusement park or a ski resort. People are wonderfully consistent. Typically, they stop at the first booth that interests them. They may even stand in a line there. Meanwhile, the people manning the booths in the back are lonely. Unless a company that interests you in front has no candidates, go directly to companies that interest you in the back of the hall. Depending on the size of the hall and the number of companies, you have about 10 minutes before other people join you. These 10 minutes can be very valuable because everyone is fresh. Later in the day, the recruiters who would rather be anywhere else may ignore you — pretty strange, huh? I've seen them pull up stakes a couple of hours early. Usually, that's when I meet the most interesting candidates because they were working in their current jobs earlier!

Would you like another secret? Introduce yourself to other job seekers. You may have run across something not interesting to you but interesting to them. Karma works! Somehow, you will benefit. They may suggest that you speak with a representative of a company that you did not intend to meet. That's why you bring extra resumes!

As you work at a career fair, it is easy to tell which companies are experienced in dealing with candidates at one. It also gives you a sense of the company. For instance, before a career fair when I am representing my clients, I walk through the hall just prior to the opening of the doors. As RecruiterGuy.com, I want to know who my true competition is for good candidates. Typically, they have arranged their booths to be welcoming to candidates. Other companies keep their tables between them and the candidates. That is commonly referred to as a barrier. Many times, how the booth is set also is a good indication of their culture. Are they open, or are they closed? Are they welcoming or not?

Generally, I try to attract one or more of my clients' managers to the fair to work with me. It is a great opportunity for them to see some of the quality of available candidates in the community and possibly even interview one or two of them. When a sharp candidate approaches, I invite them inside the booth, listen to their "Here I Am!" speech, look at their resume, and then make a quick decision on how to proceed. If they are a potential candidate for the manager who is with me, I excuse myself from the candidate for a minute to speak with the manager. The manager will look at the resume. If we agree to proceed, I suggest that the manager take the candidate to a nearby restaurant to interview. The manager is happy for an excuse to leave the booth, and the candidate is excited to have an interview so quickly. It's a win-win! More than one person has been hired that way.

Remember to pay attention as you work at the career fair. There is always the opportunity to network with companies, managers, and other attendees.

## Your Networking Toolkit

The primary tools of networking are your lists, your "Here I Am!" speech, your preparation, your perseverance, AND YOUR PASSION. There is one more very important attribute that comes into play while networking: a positive mental attitude. People do what you expect them to do; therefore, if you expect them to blow you off, your self-fulfilling expectation will cause you to say something that causes them to blow you off. Always make calls with a smile on your face and the expectation of success. It will greatly improve your success rate.

People in your network remember when you thank them — and when you don't. Think about the potential future impact. If they had a hand in your successful search for a job, please Thank them. Then ask if there anything you may do for them.

This is the time you have been waiting for. You are developing positive activity that leads to the successful completion of your search. Your four networking calls per day are giving you practice and confidence. More importantly, you are beginning to gain some success and momentum! Can interviews be far behind? You have graduated from the early items of your checklist. They are now your responsibility.

**Congratulations! You now know how to network your way to a new career! Celebrate. Put your knowledge to good use. Doing so will create opportunities to interview with companies of your choosing. Those interviews lead to offers and a new career. Celebrate this Step and put your new skills to use.**

All of this experience creates more confidence and additional threads for your branding tapestry. You are flying down the road to a new career — if you practice everything you have learned to this point.

# Job Search Process Checklist

## Preparing for Your Interviews

- ☐ Remember Joe Patten's counsel — you must **persistently** make a minimum of four networking calls (not emails nor texts) per day. More calls are better. You must be **passionate** about your career and where you may help a company be more productive and profitable. Your stories and questions must demonstrate you are the right **product** for them to buy!
- ☐ Remember Vic Method's experience where the networked jobs were more successful than the one that was not.
- ☐ Remember Kathy Loveless' professional speaking experience where 98% of her speeches were the result of referrals (i.e. networking) on the way to earning a million dollars in one year as a speaker.
- ☐ Finally, remember CEO Mark Capone's counsel that he would rather see a candidate who was referred to him from a trusted source. (NETWORKING!)
- ☐ Do you have further questions about the importance of networking in your search? I gave you a three-dimensional impact of networking on careers and on companies.
- ☐ Review the examples of the situations that required your skills. Develop a list of your positive, measurable impacts over the past 10 years, with a focus on the last five years. List them from the most recent impacts backward. After thinking about your examples over the last few days, are there better examples that you can use? As you are researching companies, new examples will continue to flow into your mind if

you allow them. Again, the format is to discuss the 4 W's: What was the challenge? What were your Analysis and Action? What was the Result? What did you Learn?

□ People remember stories, not skill lists. These stories are important to relate during your interviews.

□ Is your resume a sea of bullet points instead of your responsibilities in a paragraph and bullet points for accomplishments?

□ If you still have old annual reviews, read them for impacts that you may have forgotten. Both tasks prepare you for **Impressive Interviewing**!

□ You have developed your resume, "Here I Am!" speech, and brand as a candidate. Is your "Here I Am!" speech passionate about your experience and accomplishments? Or are you simply reciting it? If so, create a script that you may read with excitement and enthusiasm! Remember the avionics engineer's Passionate Here I Am! Speech! Begin a list of references. Decide which references are best to discuss which successful experiences.

□ Remember your goal is to find positions that you love so much that you are excited to receive compensation for your impacts. You want days to fly by. You want to make positive, measurable impacts and have fun.

□ As you network, faithfully add new names to your spreadsheet and note how they may be related to other connections. Ensure that you are only adding them once. More than one person may refer you to someone.

□ You have begun talking with people (networking). Track your results. Remember, you are in a sales process. Working in a sales process, it is important to know your numbers. While networking, it is important to track how many calls (phone and personal) you make per day. Then track the results of each call (Think baseball statistics — track measurable activity).

□ To maintain a positive mental attitude, it is important to know your averages. For instance, it is important to know that for every three calls you make, you have one conversation. For every five conversations, you get a personal meeting. For every three personal meetings, you set up an interview. For every two interviews, you receive an offer. That means 90 calls can yield an offer. If you make four calls per day, you can earn four offers over 90 days. This becomes your law of averages. Develop a spreadsheet to track:

- How many calls with no answers/left messages
- How many conversations per day
- How many names received in each conversation
- How many Introductions networking contacts set for you
- How many phone conversations created a personal meeting
- How many of those meetings set up interviews
- How many interviews resulted in offers
- How many offers extended before one was accepted

□ Analyze your results. Does it feel that your networking should yield more interviews? If so, where do your metrics seem to be lower than you expect? As you develop your averages, you may adjust your activity to speed up interviews or slow down interviews. Determine where your numbers seem low, then adjust. The tweaks may not need to be large changes, but rather small tweaks. Many times, during a job search, you will find the need to tweak approaches; and definitely, your resume to best fit the company's needs and culture

□ Redouble your networking efforts while participating in an interviewing process. **Many candidates fall into the trap of shutting down their networking activities as soon as they begin an interviewing process. They are so certain that their networking efforts are done, they quit doing the things that made them successful.** Understand that your first interviews may or may not result in offers. You may accept those offers, or you may turn them down for many reasons. Success creates more confidence. More than one offer is better than one offer! Intense networking only ends after you start your next position. Then you continue to contribute to your networks but do so outside of prime time in consideration for your new employer/business.

Celebrate your networking success daily. The celebration of your successes makes the work lighter. Every networking call adds threads to your tapestry. Your brand is developing into a recognized brand in the Employment Marketplace.

*Now that you know the how and why,*
*good luck networking!*

*You will be successful!*

*Look into your mirror three times daily*
*and read and recite:*

## I Am a Professional!
## I GOT THIS!

*Your confidence has returned.*
*You are doing a great job networking.*
*You have created some interviewing opportunities.*
*Let's ROAR into*

## Step 9 —
## Impassioned Interviewing!

## STEP 9

# IMPASSIONED INTERVIEWING

Katie is a leader and mentor. Unfortunately, during interviews, she comes across as "overqualified." She did not understand this is the company code for "not a cultural fit."

As we discussed her interviews, we practiced the eight different ways executives may structure interview questions. During that exercise, we discovered why companies did not view Katie as a cultural fit. Instead of asking interviewers, "Have you tried to handle the described situation this way?" She dove straight into her solution.

During interviews, the method to succeed is as a consultant — ask appropriate questions to research what the company has tried and failed. Then nicely probe why they felt that solution did not succeed.

A great question to ask the manager during an interview is, "What problem do you need me to help you solve?" Listen, and then ask if they tried your potential solution?

Once Katie moved to the consultative style of interviewing, she received three offers in the first week!

Two weeks ago, you wished we could do more to find your new career — and here we are! Finally, we transitioned from the marketing role of finding a job to the sales role. With 30 or more years of experience under your belt, you are in the driver's seat and are in total control of your search. Certainly, networking had a sales element — that was practice. At this point in your search, you must see that the previous steps prepared you for this moment. Embrace it!

Remember your initial assessment of your skills, experience, and attributes from Step 1? You listed the skills, experience, and attributes that you do well. Then you put an asterisk next to everything you do well that you *enjoy* doing. The next step was to create stories that demonstrated those skills and attributes in use and experience that made you proud using the 4 W's — What was the challenge? What were your analysis and action? What was the result? What did you learn? Well, it's time to pull those files out of your computer. Look at your stories. Have you improved on them? If not, how may you improve on them today? This is a recent example from my life:

> One of my skills is being an impassioned leader. Leaders lead — and we also need to improve our skills. Therefore, I applied to be a member of Leadership Park City in 2009. Myles Rademan is the Founder and Director of Leadership Park City. He modeled the program after the Kellogg Leadership program. The purpose of this program is to grow additional leaders for Park City and neighboring communities. I was not accepted. Several years later, I applied again and was accepted to be a member of Leadership Park City Class XX.
>
> Every class has a project that the group selects in one afternoon about midway through the yearlong program. What a whirlwind when 30 leaders of all ages from high school seniors to senior members of the community get together and try to determine ONE project from everyone's ideas in about two hours! Our class chose to write a kindergarten to second grade children's book. This was about one year after my first book was published. Honestly, I rolled my eyes when we decided to write, illustrate, and publish a book in five months! With 30 editors! Long story short, I was part of the team that

decided the locales in the Park City area we would highlight, others wrote stories of those locations in a poetic style, others illustrated it . . . and we ALL edited it. We had to fundraise and sell the book.

We not only sold the book; we made a nice profit that we use to give two $1,000 scholarships per year to deserving graduating Park City High School students who are headed to college. Eventually, I became a member of the Leadership Park City Alumni Association Board.

**CHALLENGE** — During the Covid-19 pandemic, our community was hurting with so many businesses closed, their employees laid off, and people getting sick. Class XX and the Leadership Park City Alumni Association decided that this was a problem that needed our attention.

**ANALYSIS and ACTION** — We analyzed the problem, looked at our funding, and decided we had sufficient funds to create a $20,000 Challenge matching grant for the Park City Community Foundation to distribute to local non-profits who support the poor and others in need.

**RESULT** — Within only three days, we raised an additional $24,430 to donate a total of $44,430!

**WE LEARNED** — Leaders lead! And others will follow our lead.

Did I demonstrate that I contributed to our community? Did we demonstrate our leadership? Does the story tell you something about me and everyone in Leadership Park City? If I were applying to a company with a social awareness program, should I tell that story? Absolutely!

What have you done in your career or volunteer experience that makes you glow? That pride builds confidence. The confidence builds enthusiasm. Top level managers prefer to hire enthusiastic and confident candidates — like you!

You now know the position you are targeting; you know which companies you would prefer to work for, and you know approximately how much money you need to earn (Salary Negotiation is our next Step).

As you network and apply for the different positions, you tailor your resume for that company and its position by using their verbiage. You need to demonstrate that you "speak their language."

On my talent attraction recruiting consulting projects, I coach my client companies that recruiting is a sales process. Remember the spreadsheet comparison where we demonstrated that the job search also mirrors the sales process in Step 3? Congratulations! You are a professional sales account representative right now! That's great if sales are your focus. Accountants are more comfortable counting money. The interviewing process is where they prove how well they count money. The same is true of all fields. What do you do well that you enjoy doing?

You worked hard to get to this point. For me, interviewing is fun. I look at it as another networking opportunity where I may be able to help a manager or company benefit from knowing me. **I define an interview as a conversation with a purpose — and both sides have the purpose of deciding if this relationship is best for them.** Think of yourself as a consultant. Learn from Katie's experience at the beginning of this Step. Prepare to ask the hiring manager leading questions so they may have the opportunity to let you know their challenges — and allow you to demonstrate you have the necessary skills and experience to assist them in meeting their goals.

This is a good time to warn you about a typical candidate's behavior. **When a candidate schedules an interview, they often stop networking. Continue networking ALL the way through your offers!** The position you are interviewing for may not be the right one. The culture may not be a fit, the offer may be too low, or you may not trust the hiring manager, etc. You do not want to have to restart your networking process and lose the momentum you've developed. So, set time aside every day to continue your networking efforts to contact four new networking contacts. In sales, action begets action; therefore, you may find more opportunities while exploring the first one. In the 25 plus years of coaching professionals, more often than not, job seekers who continue to network during the interviewing process are people who can choose between or among offers. Remember, you are looking for a career that is so enjoyable that you can't believe they are also paying you!

> During the Covid-19 pandemic, one of the director level clients I coached was networking very well. He targeted companies in his industry. He interviewed with two companies — the

first one was recently purchased by another company. When he interviewed with them, the hiring manager was a woman who worked with the firm that was purchased. She was joined by a male manager from the acquiring firm in the interview. The male was demeaning towards the woman who would be his manager during their conversation — power play. Fortunately, the person I coached recognized that treatment would most likely extend to him too.

The second company was a mature startup that was growing and had an attractive culture where goals and expectations were clearly documented.

He received an offer from both companies within an hour of each other. Of course, the offer from the first company was $90,000 and the offer from the more attractive company was $85,000. Understanding that he was probably near the top of their range, he called me and asked how he should approach the company that he really wanted to work with that offered him less compensation. He told me there were some tax credits for training he wanted that would cost him $4,000. I suggested he contact the hiring manager at the company where he wanted to work. Layout the other offer. Ask the manager if there was a way to get closer, possibly by covering the cost of the training and receiving the tax credits. The manager then extended a new offer that included that $4,000 in training — yearly. He accepted and started a week later.

This example demonstrates the importance of continuing to network while you are interviewing with another company. If he stopped with the first company, he may have felt the need to accept their offer — and be unhappy.

**I have an important little secret for you.**

As a result of working with several thousand managers since 1981, I can tell you that every single manager has one common feeling regarding interviewing, and it does not matter how skilled they are as an interviewer.

**Every single manager is rooting for you to succeed during your interview.**

Outside of recruiting teams, many managers dislike the recruiting and interviewing process. They want to spend their time managing their team and making impacts in their fields, not going through dozens of resumes and interviewing strangers. Once they have chosen a slate of candidates to interview, they hope at least one qualifies to work with them. You can understand why they do not want to begin the process again.

The best managers look at this process as an opportunity to improve their team. These are the great managers who know how to grow a high-performance team. Their interviews will be strenuous as they try to determine if you have the right skills and attitude.

Therefore, once you have been invited to interview, the odds raise in your favor that you will receive an offer to work there. You passed the first cuts.

Now it is up to you to earn the respect of the manager and/or management team. You earn this respect through preparation for the interview. If you try to skate through an interview, you may just continue skating out the door because you will lose the respect of the manager.

# Introducing A New Concept for This Book — CORE

You have the experience to succeed in interviews. You have most of the skills required, if not all of the skills. Since you incorporated positive visualization, you are more optimistic than several weeks ago. CORE will assist you to power your way through your interviews.

**C — Confidence —** The fundamentals of your search that you completed demonstrates that you are the complete package — skills, experience, and attributes to excel in this position.

**O — Optimism —** Fortunately, attitude is within your control. With your successful background, you have reason to be Optimistic.

**R — Research —** Your power move now is to research the company! Examine their website to understand as much about the company they want you to know. Conduct a Bing or Google search on both the company and the hiring manager. Look at the hiring manager's LinkedIn profile. What may you glean from their background that may be key to succeeding in the interview — same education, previous company, volunteer activities? Get to know them.

**E — Execute —** Absorb this new information. Then create a plan to use it in your interview. How will you structure questions to introduce the topics you would like to discuss with them? Execute a powerful interview.

# How Does Science Impact Interviewing?

The Science of Psychology has a major impact on this Step. The manager and their team are working to determine if you have the best skills, experience, attributes, and motivation to succeed in their position.

The Science of Sociology helps them to determine if your personality is a match for their culture. Will you fit into the team and company culture? Are you the person whose practice is to build consensus before moving forward? Or, are you the person who makes a decision and moves forward, leading other team members? Depending upon the organization's culture, one personality type may work and the other would conflict with the culture. Proper reference checks are critical to determining this cultural fit.

Computer Science combines with the other sciences during virtual and video interviews. The other area where computer science has an impact is where personality or skill assessments are required.

# Interview Preparation

Let's create a checklist. When a recruiter or manager for a company calls you for an interview, ask who will interview you and their position. If you are not aware of an opening at the company, ask what position they are considering you.

1. Go to the company's website. Comb through the website and write down pertinent questions for your side of the interview.
2. Examine their product and/or service offerings. Depending upon your experience, ask questions about their clients' needs, most popular product/service, where they expect to grow their offerings, and Where do you picture me?
3. Look at the job description. Since job descriptions notoriously are vague, try to determine the duties. Write questions regarding the job description. By the way, it may appear they will not be able to find someone with all the background they seek. They just tossed in the kitchen sink to see if they could find someone with the best experience with the faucets.

4. Search for members of the interviewing team on LinkedIn. Peruse their backgrounds. This information could be utilized to create a relationship with the manager:
5. Have they worked for the same company in their past as you?
6. Did they graduate from the same college/university?
7. Whom do you both know? Is there someone you may call to learn more about the company and the manager?
8. Do you have similar interests? Look at the interests category at the bottom of their LinkedIn profile.
9. What, if any, information is in their accomplishments category?

All this information may be used to help you create questions for your interview. Remember, Joe Patten suggested that you have more questions prepared than they have. These questions will help you determine your interest in the position, the company, and the manager with whom you will work. Additionally, your questions will demonstrate you have researched them.

## The MAGIC Question

If you are interested in the manager's expectations for you during the first year, ask the following question: What are my 3-month, 6-month, 9-month, and 12-month goals for my first year? Most managers do not think that far ahead. Amazing, huh? Yet, at the end of the 12 months, they will have to review your performance. If they throw the softball question at you — "Why do you want to know?" Your response will be, *"I like to exceed expectations. I need to know your expectations."*

## What are Standard Interview Questions?

In my experience, most managers have not been taught how to effectively interview. If they have not been taught how to effectively interview, they certainly have not been taught how to select the best qualified candidate. Not good, and that is what you face. What do they do when they need to interview candidates? They go to Human Resources and ask what questions they should ask. Human Resources will hand them a standard list of "safe" questions to ask so the company will not be sued (if the manager asks an illegal question — something that does not discuss the required duties or skills/experience for the job). These are most of the standard questions those managers receive to ask. Note, these questions are not "position specific." How do they determine who is the best fit? When I hear a manager say, this person feels good in my gut. I tell them, *"Guts are good for storing and processing food. Not so good for making hiring decisions."*

1. Tell me about yourself. Okay, many managers ask this question because this is the first time they look deeply into your resume. Other managers claim they want to see if you are prepared to answer this ubiquitous question. This should be an easy response — give your Here I Am! Speech minus "Who do you feel I should speak with next?"

2. What are your salary expectations? Fortunately, since 21 states and cities/counties prohibit companies from asking, "What is your current compensation?" many companies are changing the question to "What are your compensation expectations?" Your response is in the next Step 10 Strong Salary Negotiation! By the way, while on a recruiting contract for my client, this is my third question to a candidate.

3. Why do you want to leave your current position? This is the bridge from your Here I Am! Speech.

4. Discuss your responsibilities in your current/last position. This is where it is best to tie your experience to the company's needs. You know this from your research and your questions on what the job entails, what they expect from you, and where you may grow in the company over the next four or five years.

5. How do you handle stressful situations? Discuss a situation where your current position led you into a stressful situation. Tell a story using your 4 W's.

6. What are your strengths? Tell stories that demonstrate your strengths. Use metrics to demonstrate accomplishments. Example: "Our process improvements increased productivity by 15% and corporate profitability by 10%."

7. Where do you feel you need improvement? Or you may hear, what is your weakness? The best way to respond is to be truthful. Example:

"One of my weaknesses is the ability to speak effectively in front of groups." Then show you are doing something to strengthen that weakness. "Since I recognize that needs strengthening, I am attending Toastmasters and learning to improve my presentation skills."

I have a story for that question.

One client asked me to train a talented new human resource representative on how to interview. We chose an executive administrative assistant position that reported to a tough sales vice president. The rep combed through the resumes we sourced and picked the three she thought were best. When I looked at the stack, I concurred. She set up the appointments for the three candidates.

When each of them arrived, she introduced me to them. I mentioned that I was coaching the rep to improve her interviewing skills. I was going to be on the other side of the conference room table from them. If we went through the entire interview without me asking a question, that was great. If I did ask a question, it was because I needed additional clarification.

The first two candidates and the rep did just fine. I did not feel the need to speak up. The third candidate was doing well until she was asked what her weakness was. The candidate said, "My weakness is that I like people too much." Well, that was the first time that I ever heard that as a weakness, so she received my full attention. She then went on to make her weakness a strength.

The rep was going to let her move forward. I decided to probe a little deeper. I excused myself and said, "Well, we were looking more for a skill you needed to improve. What you did was turn your weakness into a strength. I recognize that approach in interview coaching. Can you tell me what area you need to improve?" She responded, "Another weakness is that . . . ." and proceeded to turn it into a strength. I replied that I understood how she was taking some attribute, discussing it as a weakness, and then demonstrating positive results from that action or attribute.

Trying one more time, I asked, "This is an important support position to a vice president of sales. Are there any software classes where you would like to improve your skills or any other area we could help you improve your skills?" Her response? "I am NOT a weak person!" She was right! However, she did not listen, either. I apologized profusely and turned the conversation back over to the rep. The rep recognized that the interview was essentially over at that point since we found her fatal flaw.

8. Discuss a time you were put into a difficult position — what steps did you take to handle the situation? Tell a story using your 4 W's.
9. Discuss why you feel we should hire you? Use your research to demonstrate you have the skills, experience and are prepared to be successful in this new position

# Humans Remember Stories

My belief is humans are hardwired to remember stories back to the time when we first began to develop language. I picture the first humans scavenging the area around their cave or protected area to sleep. When they went hunting for food, whether it was vegetation or small animals, they remembered the location. When they returned to their community, they communicated where the field was located: "Go down this path, cross the stream at the bottom of the hill, follow the direction of the water, the vegetation is on this side (pointing to their right side)." This was a way we survived as a species — and why we are hardwired to remember stories.

Therefore, during your interviews, it is important to relate your experience in short stories.

When I was on a recruiting contract with a major telecommunications firm, the managers were interviewing six candidates per day. Many times, they later referred to a candidate by "She was the candidate that told the story about . . ." Soon, another manager who interviewed candidates that day would chime in, "That's Trina!" And everyone agreed. Then one would ask to extend Trina an offer.

# 8 Different Ways I Structure Interview Questions

In my talent attraction recruiting business, I pre-screen all candidates before forwarding them to my client manager. Prior to pre-screening, I forward my proposed questions to the hiring manager. My request is they review the proposed questions for my interview, suggest any additional questions, and if they want me to delete any questions.

These are the eight different ways I may structure interview questions. Many times, since most managers have not been trained on how to effectively interview, my interview is the most rigorous — and candidates tell me so. Feel free to draw from these examples once you land a position and need to interview candidates.

## 1. *Behavioral Questions*

Much has been written about **behavioral interviewing**. Some companies attempt to design the entire interview as a behavioral interview. People are wonderfully predictive. When backed into a corner, we attempt to solve a problem in the same manner where we found success in the past. We will attempt to solve similar challenges the exact same way until someone gets . . . 4 and hits us upside the head saying, "You can't do that anymore!" The interviewer anticipates challenges the new employee will face in this position and structures a question that can give insight into how the candidate will handle the situation.

For instance, let's assume that this is a call-center manager position with angry clients who escalate after getting unsatisfactory answers. Here's a potential line of behavioral questions for a professional with call-center experience: "When you were a manager at XYZ Services Co., how did you handle angry clients who wanted to escalate a problem up the chain of responsibility? Can you give me a couple of examples when you were able to satisfy the client?" After you respond they may ask, "Obviously, it is difficult to satisfy everyone. Please give me an example of a situation when you couldn't satisfy the client. Describe the situation, the actions that you took, and the results. What did you learn from that situation?" You can tell that they are trying to determine how you will respond to those clients once you start working there. More importantly, they demonstrated the best way to create a story.

A follow-up question generally is the most effective way to probe a candidate's response to a behavioral question. There are several methods to probe the response. One way is to compliment them. "Congratulations on handling that very difficult situation! What experience from your past did you draw from to decide to take that path?"

## 2. One-Step Question

Occasionally, it is good for the manager to change the line of questioning by asking a probing type of question where the interviewer is looking for a what, when, where, or who response. **This is the one-step question.** For instance, "Where were you working when you were trained to handle conflict?"

## 3. The Two-Step Question

It is best if the manager pays attention to your response to any question. **Asking a follow-up question (making this a two-step question)** to your response to the probing question can provide more information that leads to understanding your motivations. An example follow-up question to the one above could be, "If you were receiving such valuable conflict training at that company, why did you choose to leave?" Or they are looking for more information. They may want to see how much information you have absorbed in your research and interview, so they ask, "What positive, measurable impacts do you feel you could make in this position?"

## 4. Pause/Silence

Up until now, you may have felt that I was a nice guy. Actually, your assessment is true ... until I am interviewing you. Then I am still nice but this way of structuring a question makes most candidates uncomfortable. Understand that most people are uncomfortable with silence during communications. I experience this when I speak to audiences and pause so a point sinks in. You will hear a cough or some other sound in different areas of the audience. It is ESPECIALLY true during an interview. People feel the need to fill the silence with a sound.

My method is to ask them a behavioral question about midway through the interview, so they have become accustomed to a certain cadence. When the candidate begins to respond to my question, I smile and nod encouragingly. When they feel they are finished, I continue smiling and nodding my head — and add rolling my hand as if to say silently, "Please continue . . ."

On several occasions, the candidate continued to talk for 10 minutes without asking me for clarification. One candidate reached the 22-minute point and stopped dead in his tracks. He looked at me and said, "I just blew this interview, didn't I?" Generally, they end up telling me things they should have kept to themselves.

When you find yourself in this situation, simply ask the interviewer what additional information they are looking for, so your response may be focused on their need for information. An interview is not the time to enter the confessional, especially unknowingly.

## 5. What Is the Same/What Is Different?

These questions may be used to identify how you handle different corporate cultures, manager styles, or challenges. Therefore, they may ask you to differentiate your experiences between or among former employers. An example could be, "You said that the sale to XYZ Company was one of the most complicated sales you have closed. How did that compare to the one with ABC Company? How were they different? What did you learn from each sale?"

## 6. Example

This method of structuring a question is for the interviewer to take an example from their experience — and then ask the candidate if they have a similar experience. An example could be: There have been a couple of times in my experience when two co-workers conflicted. That conflict makes me feel uncomfortable. Tell me about a time when you felt the same. How did you handle that situation?

## 7. Echo

There are times that the interviewer may repeat some of the words from your answer to elicit a response. Your response to why you left a position could be, "I just didn't feel that my professional impacts were appreciated." The interviewer may respond, "Professional impacts?" They are allowing you to talk about your impacts and, at the same time develop a better understanding of your motivations.

## 8. *Yes/No Questions*

In my talent attraction recruiting business, I help my clients attract all levels of new employees — executive to labor. When it comes to Yes/No question responses, candidates who are not polished executives are the most fun because they sometimes have no filters. Examples of questions when interviewers are simply looking for a yes or no response are: Have you been convicted of a felony? *One laborer responded, "No, but." I asked, "BUT What?" He answered, "I was charged with assault and battery with a firearm, but my lawyer got me off."* Not good. If the employees may need to drive a company vehicle, another question could be, "Do you have a current clean driver's license? *Many times, laborers responded, "Yes but" . . . (generally that means the license is not clean) When I ask what does "BUT" mean? Their response was, "Well, I got a ticket for running a red light last week. I tell them their record is not clean. They responded, "But we haven't gone to court yet . . ."* Noted.

# Different Interviewing Formats

1. Phone or Zoom Interviews (also known as phone screens). These interviews may take different paths:

   A. The corporate recruiter interviews you asking you pretty basic screening questions, including the ubiquitous how much would you like to earn? (Don't answer that yet! Wait until the next Step!). Then they decide whether to introduce you to the hiring manager. Quoting a dollar number may make that an easier decision for them.

   B. The recruiter sets up an invitation to link to one of several remote software video interviews that generally last 15 to 30 minutes. In these video interviews, the recruiter will ask a series of questions related to the job. You may have a do over if you like. Here are some thoughts on how to best handle these interviews.

1. Check your background before your interview by going to Skype.com or Zoom.com and checking the video. In my office, I prefer a backdrop instead of a green screen. Ensure that your lighting is towards your face instead of behind your head. Sometimes, depending upon the lighting, it is best to close blinds or curtains.

2. Practice looking directly at your camera. The person reviewing your interview will feel that you are looking directly at them. An IT professional (of course) recommends that you put a PostIt on the top of your monitor with an arrow pointed directly at the camera.

3. Practice looking confident while interviewing.

Then the manager reviews your video interview at their leisure before deciding to formally interview you.

C. The hiring manager interviews you over the phone. Generally, these interviews will run in one of two ways. The first is a half hour interview to determine if they wish to invite you to a personal interview. The second path may be a full-blown, hour-long interview with the hiring manager deciding to move you to their executive before a personal interview. This was the path my cyber-security firm client took for their sales professional openings.

D. The hiring manager and other members of the team interview you via videoconferencing software (Zoom, Teams, Skype, GoToMeeting, Webex, etc.). These interviews in the Covid-19 world may lead to offers. It will be interesting to follow whether companies choose to make this their practice instead of flying remote candidates in for personal interviews. (A story about a recent executive candidate illustrates this point in the next chapter.) Beware of your background! Green screens do not always mask what is behind you!

Last week, I met with the CEO of a young company. She related the story of a recent Zoom interview with a sharp female candidate. Two of her executives joined her for the interview. At the beginning of the interview, they noticed the candidate used a green screen. The interview proceeded well until . . . a shirtless male with shorts walked behind her, appearing in and out of the screen. She and her executives glanced at each other as if to say, "Did you see that?" A couple of minutes later, the same shirtless male walked back behind the candidate.

It is important to be aware of your background — and make others aware of your interview, especially in your home!

E.  You are invited to a formal personal interview, either locally or brought in from out of town. Depending upon the level of position, for instance, the executive level, you may be invited to an interview with the "search team" of the board of directors of the company.

# Personal Interview Formats

Most professionals are familiar with the "normal" (norms may differ among companies) manager and candidate interview, sitting across the desk in an office or across the table in a conference room. Depending upon the nature of the manager, this interview may take the form of a grilling or a semiformal conversational interview. Companies that value a cultural fit will often require that the hiring manager add people from other departments to the interview team. These additional interviewers are staff that you will interface with in your position. This is your opportunity to build a personal relationship with the manager and interviewing team by telling those great 4 W's stories!

## *1. One on One Interview*

This interview has you and your interviewer one on one. In many ways, this is my favorite interview. It allows you and your interviewer to build a relationship in a short period, usually 30 to 40 minutes. Tell your stories to demonstrate you have the skills, experience, and motivation to not only do the job but to exceed expectations. Ensure you ask relevant questions based on your research. Near the end of your interview, ask the manager if they have any concerns about your ability to be a successful member of the team — best to get any objections on the table. You may say, "I understand your concern. We probably did not go into enough depth about how my experience and skills would enable me to be successful. I am very interested in working with you in this position. Would you like me to tell you another story to demonstrate how my skills from ABC Company would transfer here?" As you prepare to leave the interview, ask the manager, "What are the next steps?" If the manager tells you to expect a decision by next Tuesday, tell them again, "I am very interested in this position. If I don't hear from you by next Tuesday, may I reach out to you on Wednesday?" (You are receiving permission to contact them again).

## 2. The Panel Interview

More companies are selecting the panel interview as the favorite interviewing tool. All three company employees/managers hear the question asked and the candidate's response. The panel interview also potentially places the candidate under a little stress. In this format, the managers many times will ask a question at the same time to increase pressure. The best practice is to ask the person who asked the tougher question if you may answer the other question first. Generally, they will agree. This gives your brain a little more time to process the more difficult question in the background while you are responding to the other question. Then turn to the other interviewer and ask if they would please ask their question again. Totally focus on that person. Handle the end of the interview the same way as the one-on-one interview. Ask, "Do you have any concerns about my candidacy?" If so, ask where they have a concern. Before leaving, tell them you are very interested in their position. Ask "What are the next steps?" Then ask for permission to contact them again as you do in the other interview format.

## 3. The Half Circle Format

This was new to me in Utah. I was coaching a system administrator candidate. He told me about his interview experience with one company. About 20 candidates for different positions were given an interview at the same time with assorted managers from the same company. They were directed to sit in any one of the chairs in a semi-circle, in no particular order. My client picked a spot in the middle of the semi-circle, figuring they were going to start at one end or the other. Then he paid attention to which questions were asked each candidate. By the time they arrived at his seat, he was prepared. He did well. They extended him an offer the next day that he accepted.

## 4. *The Competitive Interview*

This is another interview format that introduces stress to the candidate's interviewing experience. In this format, the candidates have passed their previous knowledge and experience-based interviews. Now the company is down to the cultural best fit decision. Several executive candidates sign a non-disclosure saying they will not reveal the other two candidates. The three candidates sit across a conference table from the executive team and a psychologist. The executive team has four primary objectives:

1. How does each candidate respond to the other candidate's interview responses (best not to roll your eyes!!)?
2. How do the candidates respond to critiques of their response by the executive team?
3. Do the candidates respect each other in the thick of the interview?
4. Would I want them to join us as a member of the executive team?

Some executives swear by this final interview because of their success utilizing it. Personally, I never participated in one of these interviews. It would have been interesting. However, I did propose it once for one of my clients when we were down to the last two candidates for an audit position. My sense was one of the candidates may have a little too sharp an edge for the team.

> The Director of Internal Audit and I discussed the format and how I would present it to the two final candidates. He liked the idea and prepared to move forward by including several of his managers in the interview. When I sent the invite and fully described the format, I received two replies. The first internal auditor welcomed the opportunity to participate in an "interesting interview format." The second response was very

different — and truly not unexpected. This candidate decided to respond to the email invitation in all caps — not recommended. The response went something like this . . . THIS TYPE OF INTERVIEW IS ILLEGAL BY THE SHRM (Society for Human Resource Management) RULES. I WILL NOT PARTICIPATE IN ILLEGAL INTERVIEWS. Well, okay then. This is called a voluntary disqualification. (As a SHRM member, I can certify this type of interview format, while seldom utilized, is legal.) I called him and apologized for his discomfort. Then I let him know we had no further interest in his candidacy.

The candidate's response to our interview explanation and invitation verified my feelings about how he would act in the field when his views were challenged. We selected the better candidate of the two.

## Personal Interview Day Preparation

Congratulations! Today's the day you shine! You are prepared for anything the interviewing team can throw at you. Be confident! You are prepared. You have the opportunity to review your research on the company, the team on LinkedIn, products/services, and company news from Bing/Google/company website. You've developed questions for the interviewing team on the company, their processes, where they feel pain, and where they picture you in your role. You took time to practice your responses to questions earlier in this Step and here — Potential Interview Questions — RecruiterGuy

Now you feel nicely confident and are prepared for a friendly match of wits. Remember, the manager secretly wants you to succeed.

If you smoke, do not smoke that day. Ensure you wear clothes cleaned by a dry cleaner and are fresh. Nonsmokers can smell smoke on your breath and your clothes. Do not kid yourself. I can smell smoke on clothing, even if you were not the one smoking. Today, smoking can cost you a job offer. Like it or not, insurance research demonstrates that smokers are sick more often. Companies may select the candidates who are the best "fit" for their business. You make your own decisions.

# The Clothes Make the Man and Woman

If the job is an office or sales job, wear professional clothing: suit, tie, polished shoes. Women should wear conservative jewelry (no dangling earrings) and conservative cosmetics if they decide to wear either. Beyond earrings, it is best not to show body piercings or tattoos in a professional office for your interview. You may always dress in office casual once you start your new job if that is the company culture.

You have heard this before — **you have one opportunity to make a good first impression.**

It is natural for people to look at your clothing and accessories and make judgments regarding your "fit" in an organization. I've heard candidates say, "If they don't like my beard/long hair/tattoos/piercings, that's tough. That's who I am." I accept that line of thinking. Just do not complain if the company feels another person is a better fit for your other-  wise perfect job. Remember, the manager also has a right to determine if someone is a fit for their team. For more information on the topic of the importance of dressing to impress, watch my 116th television interview — www.youtube.com/ watch?v=tBEIx7hXoWE&t=11s

> One of my consumer product group clients hired a human-re- source generalist. Their corporate culture shuns body piercings and tattoos. They inform candidates during the interviewing process that they are not acceptable. The can- didate interviewed without a tongue stud; however, on her first day on the job, she was sporting a tongue stud. The vice president of human resources requested that she remove it. The new employee, who was on a customary 90-day proba- tion refused to remove it. That was also her last day.

A great book, if you have questions about dressing for an interview, is John T. Molloy's *Dress for Success*. He researched professional dress- ing and how people reacted to different styles. I have recommended his books to candidates for more than 25 years because they are based on research and fact.

If it is an outside job — construction, for example — wear appropriate, clean business casual clothing to your interview. If the job is with a company that values outdoor experience, wear appropriate clothing for the position.

> I worked a career fair once in the Midwest where a candidate told his friends that he was so good and companies were so desperate for candidates, he could even get a job offer if he walked around with a clown costume on. What an arrogant schmuck! He even dropped off his resume with companies while dressed in the costume. No offers for him then — nor probably later. His arrogance really stood out. By the way, the companies who received his resume shared his name with other companies.

Beware of the food that you eat a couple of hours before your interview. Some food can make you gassy. (Or smelly!)

> Once when we were interviewing IT professionals, the IT manager came to my office when her interview with a candidate was over. The manager said, "Don't ever put someone like that in front of me again!" I was startled. The candidate worked for a competitor and on the same types of systems. At that point, we did not know he was failing the technical test. I asked the manager what was wrong with the candidate. It seemed that shortly after he sat down, the poor guy began having gas problems. The manager had to open her windows when he left. Lesson learned.

## Courtesy Counts

If you will be even two minutes late, call ahead and tell your connection (HR or the hiring manager). They understand construction, accidents, flat tires, etc. Where did that courtesy go? Everyone has a cell phone now! (Speaking of cell phones, turn them off before you enter the building.) Respect other people and they will respect you.

Have you ever had a candidate simply no show for an interview with the CEO? No call. Silence. One of my client CEOs called me 30 minutes after the candidate was supposed to show up. **He was disappointed that I did not let him know that candidate decided not to interview.** I had no clue he decided not to interview with the CEO. When I called the candidate to ask him why he no-showed, he said he heard bad things about the CEO and decided not to go to the interview. He did not call me to let me know because he "was afraid you would try to talk me into going to my scheduled interview." Excuse me? This is the best way I know to get on a do not call list.

Sure enough, 10 years later he applied for a position with my then current client in Chicago. He requested a conversation. We spoke. I asked him about his experience since the last time we spoke. This time, his experience was not close to what I was searching for — and I told him so. Several days later, the VP from my client called me. HE called HER and complained I refused to introduce him. She was not surprised when I told her why he was not qualified. Then I told the story about the CEO. Now he will never be recruited by me nor her.

Please always call if you decide to cancel an interview. If you do not, the result may impact your career far worse than you may imagine. His decision still impacts his career.

When you walk into the office for your interview, treat everyone with respect. Period. I generally ask everyone in the reception area to tell me if the candidate was disrespectful. This is the time you should be on your best behavior. Respect the receptionist and act professionally through your interviews. I occasionally have had candidates who felt they were too important to listen to requests the receptionist made. Those actions rarely go unnoticed. The receptionist will let people in the company know if you were not respectful. You would think this would not have to be said. However . . .

Occasionally, you will interview with a company that prefers candidates to complete and sign the application in their office. There have been times when a candidate refused to complete the application when the receptionist presented it. I'm not sure what one expects to gain from that refusal. It sure isn't going to be a ringing endorsement. A candidate once did not complete the application before the interview as requested. Preceding his interview, the HR manager "allowed" him to complete the application at her desk as she waited and worked on e-mail. That experience was probably a little uncomfortable . . . he did not receive an offer. He was probably lucky he still had an interview.

Here comes your first interviewer. Approach with confidence, appropriate eye contact, and a friendly smile. Give them a firm handshake — do not break their fingers, just firm. Never give anyone a wet fish handshake! Yuck! It just says so many bad things about you — lack of confidence is among them. It used to surprise me when a woman gave me a firm handshake. Now women seem to be taught the importance of a firm handshake and do so more consistently than some men.

Appropriate eye contact means to look directly at the interviewer, but this is not a staring contest. A nice friendly smile is appropriate. It is fine to accept an offer of water. Water is preferable because it can help settle your throat should it tighten. Remember that coffee may leave your mouth dry and with that nasty used coffee smell. I know. I drink coffee.

When you go into the office or conference room, wait until your interviewer indicates where you should take a seat before sitting. *Once I had a manager candidate that I was interviewing go behind the desk when we entered the office. I smiled and said, "I can see what side of the desk you are used to sitting." He laughed and said, "Oops!" He was fine. I let him remain in that seat for our interview. We offered the job and he accepted.* Generally, the interviewer should gesture toward the appropriate seat.

When you have a cup or container of water, ask for a coaster before placing it on a desk. It is not good form to stain a nice desk, but you would be remembered.

In preparation for your interviews, visualize the potential structure of your interview. There generally is a warm-up period where some small talk occurs, followed by "tell me about yourself." It is followed by the meat of the interview, and then the point where the manager has decided; and asks if you have any further questions. Professionals pay attention during interviews, and sense when you are moving into the different phases. Many times, you may know if the manager is definitely interested in you. The manager may just tell you so and ask when you can start. They may be more subtle, but still, let you know there is interest in your candidacy.

When I present "The Secrets of a Successful Job Search," I tell the audience that a good interview is like a racquetball game. In advance of playing a racquetball game, you have a short warm-up session. It allows an experienced player to test the opposing player. Just as in the racquetball warm-up, the first questions in the interview are very easy: "Tell me a little about your experience." Generally, the interviewer asks this question while they are reading your resume (sometimes for the first time). This is an appropriate time to use your "Here I Am!" speech. Then they may ask a little about your most recent job. Now that you are warmed up, a skillful interviewer will begin the behavioral questions mixed in with the specific skill questions.

Look at pictures and certificates or degrees on their office walls. Imagine your good fortune if you happen to note they graduated from the same college as you. This gives you an immediate relationship with them. Possibly there is a familiar travel photo or trophy in the office, anything that allows you to relate.

One or more of the questions may be directed toward your relationship with your previous managers. If you are so inclined, this would be a great opportunity to absolutely slam them. Do not do it! Just be happy to characterize your relationship as "professional." If you say negative things about a previous manager, what happens?

The hiring manager wonders if the problem was the manager or you. Then they wonder what you will say about them in a couple of years. This is not the path you want them on. Do not lie and say you had a wonderful relationship if it was not. Remember, the previous manager may be called as a reference. When the previous manager asks the hiring manager how you characterized the relationship and the reply is "professional," they will probably return the favor.

> I once worked with a senior manager who laid out a situation in her interview. If the candidate did not ask a specific question, she would not extend an offer to them. (She never shared with me what the specific question was). You need to be an active listener. If you can focus on the hiring manager and their questions, it is a good idea to jot down some notes. These may help you develop questions. Remember,

> if you do not understand how an organization is set up or why a company has a specific process, or why something that you heard sounded wrong, ask the interviewers a question to clarify your thinking. That is more than okay; it is expected. Remember to ask good, informed questions based on your notes and based on what the manager has told you.

Part of your job during the interview is to attempt to build a professional relationship with the people who conduct the interview. Remember, if someone is interviewing you, they generally have input on whether you will be hired. Most hiring managers want to feel that you will jump into their canoe and paddle upstream with them. You build that relationship through active listening and asking good questions — and through the stories that you relate that demonstrate you have done this in the past.

During the interview, it is a good idea to take notes. Focus on the challenges and where you may be able to make impacts. It is good to discuss an area where you must make an impact. Once you feel the manager is comfortable that you will make that impact, ask him or her if he or she agrees you will be able to make progress there. This reinforces in their minds that they have found someone who can help solve problems. Isn't that what people are paid for — solving problems? If he agrees, then write it down. If not, you now know that you must overcome that objection before you receive an offer. Ask if you can return to that question or situation and discuss it further. At this point, you are consulting with him. Ask for more information and then use an experience from your past that demonstrates you can make that impact or know how to solve the problem.

## Posture Check

Your posture during an interview is very important. If you lean back in your chair, it appears you lack interest in the conversation. Sit toward the edge of your chair and sit straight up. When you make a point, lean forward to demonstrate the importance of that point.

This action also demonstrates your confidence in making the point. This confidence, shown by a professional, gives you the edge over someone who is not confident. Over the years, many candidates have lost opportunities because managers felt they were either lazy or not interested. Their posture gave a bad impression.

## Business Meals As A Culture Check

Candidates for consulting or executive positions may be invited to lunch or dinner with the team. The purpose is to measure your fit as a member of the team in a social situation. They may wait until you have food in your mouth to ask you a question (and yes, it is intentional). How do you respond? Hopefully, you nod and gesture that you will finish chewing before you respond. Please, never spray someone with a mouth full of food! Over lunch, even if offered, never accept any alcohol to drink. This is a test of your "normal practice."

You, or you and your Spouse/Significant Other, may be invited to dinner with other executives and spouses. It is best to ask what the dress expectations are. If you are in Baltimore, a suit probably will not be appropriate at a crab feast. The purpose is to measure how well you integrate socially with the other members — and by extension, their clients. Wait to see how others respond to the offers of a drink before you do. If you decide on a drink, nurse that drink for the entire meal.

Remember CORE. If they invite you to a meal, they want to hire you. Act Confident and be friendly. Be Optimistic during the meal. Your Research may help you decide on alcohol or no alcohol (based on their religion or acts). Now Execute a wonderful time with this team.

## Wrapping Up and Reference Checks

As you interview, you are measuring the company, the hiring manager, and the position in real time. Once both of you have completed your interview, you probably know your level of interest. This is a great time to tell the hiring manager that you are interested in the position because "I feel . . . (give him or her some solid reasons regarding the job duties, the manager's management style, and/or the company's culture)." As you leave (if you are interested in the position), it is a good time to ask: "Is there anything that would prevent you from offering this position to me?" Why do you ask that question? If you are interested in the job, that question will tell you if there is information that you need to explain, either in a different way or in a bit more detail, and satisfy the hiring manager's objection.

You know you just had a great interview when you emerge from the interview sweating and smiling!

Your brain plays games with you sometimes. Once you get 15 to 20 minutes away from the interview, you will begin to remember aspects of the conversation that I refer to as the "Wish I Would Have Saids." Find a quiet place — a restaurant or café where you can order a soda or coffee, a library or park, or even your own car — to sit down and make some notes about your conversation/conversations. This is an important exercise for several reasons.

1. Most people cannot prepare so completely for an interview as to be prepared to give the best examples for each skill within the context of a new company.

2. If you do not write them down, I guarantee that you will remember that you had "Wish I Would Have Saids," but to save your life, you cannot remember a single one. If you get a second interview with the company, this new information should be mentioned. It can mean the difference between an offer or not. If there is no second interview, this information may be used for negotiation if a lower-than-expected offer is extended. We will cover that in the salary negotiation chapter coming up.

3. Finally, do you want to differentiate yourself from the other candidates? Sit down and handwrite a personal thank you note to each person who participated in the interview. You may mail your thank you notes or drop them off at the company. Sending an email is a nice touch too. Unfortunately, it may get caught in the company spam folder. Sadly, today most candidates forget that common courtesy. People remember when you take this extra step.

Now let us discuss how to impress with your references. **A very strong reference can make the difference between receiving an offer that you will absolutely accept and not receiving an offer.**

Enlightened companies and hiring managers understand the importance of an effective reference check. Do not let people tell you that reference checking is dead. Too many times I have heard managers say the reference check is a waste of time. Legally, it may be regaining importance as the final due diligence before hiring a candidate. Reference checks certainly have a role in determining cultural fit. Therefore, it is important to be able to contact at least three people who can discuss you as an employee or the different skills you have demonstrated. Companies usually require three professional references who can intelligently discuss your professional abilities.

> I once interviewed a female programmer/analyst. Her responses demonstrated that she knew what she was doing professionally. She offered me several references. So, I called her most recent reference, a female manager, and mentioned that the candidate had given me her name as a reference. When the manager burst out laughing, I thought, "That is not a good sign!"
>
> The manager asked me if I had met the candidate in person. I replied that I had. She said, "You probably noticed that she was gorgeous." I replied that I did. The manager said she had hired the candidate. She was very talented; however, after working there for a short period, she began to date one of her coworkers. After an intimate relationship that lasted several months, she broke off the relationship — and began dating another coworker. Evidently, she whispered some of her previous relation's interesting preferences to her new friend.
>
> Shortly after, the manager found the two males fist fighting in the hall over this woman. All three were looking for new jobs after the fight.

This was not a person I would introduce to a client. Be sure to check with your references before giving their names to a potential employer. If they are excited to be a reference, that is a great sign. If they are reticent, it is best to move on. It is a good idea to coach a reference just prior to the call from either a manager or human resources representative. How do you coach a reference? As an active listener during your interview, you generally can tell if the manager is concerned about your ability to professionally perform one or more of the required duties of a position. Suggest to the reference that they bring up a specific success that you had while working with them to demonstrate that skill, especially if the manager does not ask the question. "May I tell you about the time that ____ solved a major problem for our team?" References appreciate this type of guidance. Otherwise, they are trying to remember examples that may be several years or more in the past.

The references that you choose to discuss your abilities should be people who have seen you successfully perform related, required duties while working with them. Therefore, one reference may be able to discuss your management capabilities. Another reference may be able to focus on your technical abilities. (In this case, "technical" means your day-to-day functions, whether you are a nurse, recruiter, CFO, writer, mechanic, or software engineer.) The final reference may focus on your strategic abilities (project planning, long-term planning, budgeting, etc.). Management references are the best. Sales or sales-support professionals may want to use one or more clients as references. Just be careful if this is a confidential search.

When you forward your references for a position, note where the person may be able to give the best feedback on your abilities. This information will help coach the person conducting the reference check. All references need to be able to discuss your fit within their organizations and whether they would hire you again.

There are occasions when you may want to leverage a written reference letter preceding an interview. Let's say a manager whom you networked with feels that you may not have the necessary experience for their position. If that reference letter refers to that related experience and praises your success, you would be well served if you offered to forward the letter to the manager. It could make the difference between setting an interview or losing out.

Once you reach this point in the series of processes, you are nearing a successful conclusion to your search.

What is the value of every single interview? Every interview adds more threads to the tapestry of your brand. More importantly, you learn with each interview what is creating resonance and what is not. All this practice leads you to your accepted offer.

**For a list of potential interview questions, see here — https://recruiterguy.com/interview-questions/**

# Job Search PROCESS Checklist — Impressive Interviewing

☐ Your skills assessment is done; however, it is a dynamic document that may change according to your memory and the jobs you locate. Certainly, add to your list when former co-workers remind you of success stories from your experience with them.

☐ Your base resume is completed. You change your resume to reflect the needs of each company that you either apply to or interview with.

☐ You continue to network and grow your networking contacts — especially after you have set up interviews. Keep your networking momentum going!

☐ In preparation for each interview (even second interviews with the same company), research the company and review your notes. What challenges can you help the team or company overcome?

☐ You have reviewed the different interviewing formats.

☐ You have practiced the different interviewing methods to be confident in your responses to different styles of questions. Prepare for the interview by reviewing the list of potential interview questions here — https:// recruiterguy.com/interview-questions/

☐ You checked to ensure your cell phone is off. It is embarrassing when it rings during an interview. If you answer it, you probably will not receive an offer.

☐ Remember to ask the manager about the 3-month, 6-month, 9-month, and 12-month goals early in the conversation.

☐ You have developed responses to both your strengths and weaknesses questions.

☐ As the interview is coming to completion, you tell the manager that you are interested in the position — and why.

☐ Prepare a list of potential references before your interview. Some may be former managers. Others may be able to discuss certain technical skills (nursing procedures, sales skills, programming skills, etc.)

☐ After your conversation, go somewhere quiet and list your "Wish I Would Have Saids." These are better examples than the ones you used during the interview. You may use these examples in second interviews and salary negotiations.

*This is a natural segue into the next chapter —*

## STEP 10 —
## Strong Salary Negotiation

*I AM A PROFESSIONAL!*

*I GOT THIS!*

## STEP 10

# *STRONG SALARY NEGOTIATION*

> Kristi is a sharp project manager. She wanted to expand her horizons with a new company — and she had the company where she wanted to work in her sights. She found someone to introduce her to the company. She was excited, and a little scared because salary negotiation was not one of her strengths. I coached her this far — and coached her on strong salary negotiation.
>
> She followed my advice and excitedly called me after accepting an offer that was 30% above her current compensation!

Kristi was one of eleven professionals that I coached during Covid-19 who accepted substantially higher offers than their previous compensation . . . so far!

The Science of Psychology strongly influences your actions during Salary Negotiation. Are you confident with your skills, experience, and attributes as they apply to this new Career? Are you confident in your negotiating abilities? Remember, the ability to negotiate is part of every position. How well do you negotiate with other team members to pull their weight? This is the time to negotiate to benefit you and your family.

Generally, job seekers feel angst when it comes to salary negotiation. See? I just had to mention it and you tightened up. It is understandable. Few people have been taught the ebbs and flows of negotiating a new compensation package. Note: I said compensation package. Sometimes those packages include bonuses, benefits, stock options, and other ways to benefit your lifestyle. This Step teaches you all you need to know about speaking with a future employer about compensation, what to say — and more importantly what NOT to say — to generate the best offer for your services. It is like a recipe — simply follow the directions. Remember, on the recruiting side of my business, I AM the person you initially speak with and negotiate your compensation.

When do salary negotiations informally begin for a company? Don't they informally begin when the manager and executives agree on a needed role and attach a budget range for the position? When do salary negotiations informally begin for you? They begin when you decide on your next role and the compensation package you require.

How many times have you successfully negotiated a satisfactory level of compensation for your career? Many people I coached would reply, "I guess I did okay." That does not sound "Great" nor even "satisfactory"! If you have worked for the same company for 30 years, you may never have negotiated salary. The company offered you a salary package that you accepted. Then you received the 2% to 3% annual increase — "but hey, I'm employed . . ."

With all your years of experience, what are your skills worth for your current company? (hint . . . they tell you every paycheck) What are your skills worth for other companies? Your worth depends on many factors. Have your skills and experience grown every year? Or are you a professional who has repeated the same job for 11 years? That is certainly a comfortable plan . . . and it has increased your value to neither your current employer nor a potential new employer.

Other factors include:

- What is the employment economy — up or down?
- How in demand are your skills?
- What new skills have you picked up in the last 4 years?
- Are you a lifelong learner?
- Are you a person who successfully learned new skills and risen through the ranks? (Hopefully!)

Every company is different, even in the same industry. Many value positions differently. Salary negotiation is also an area where executives have more leverage than most mid-level professional candidates — however, everyone SHOULD take advantage of lessons learned in this Step. I include a negotiating script later in this chapter that has proven to be valuable for all professionals.

Salary negotiation is a skill rarely taught. Remember your college/university years. Did your professors ever teach you salary negotiation? If so, based on what experience? Did they read a book like this and become an expert? Likely and unlikely. Likely they read the book; unlikely they negotiated a compensation package beyond what was offered them unless their research attracts lots of money to the institution. In many cases, professors are public employees of a state government.

Have any companies taught you salary negotiation? Not likely. "What? To leave us and make more money?"

As an expert talent attraction professional, I know a little about salary negotiation from both sides of the desk. Make sense? Of course, it does. Would you like to improve your compensation package negotiation skills? If the answer is yes, continue reading. Later in this Step, I will give you a cadence and script to use that has proven highly successful for job seekers I have coached for 35 years.

Let us lay a foundation first. We will work through the basics and logically create your plan. Then we will build to the cadence and script.

You need to create a spreadsheet similar to the one below. Your decision on an offer needs to be rational, not a hasty, emotional decision. Too often, professionals get caught up with, "I NEED A Job!" without calculating if they may afford that job and offer.

In your first column list salary, bonuses (Sign-on, Performance, Annual, Profit Sharing, etc.), 401(k), health benefits, PTO/vacation/sick leave, car, cell phone, Work from Home benefits (High Speed Internet, Landline Phone, Computer, Printer, other office equipment, etc.), and any other potential benefits (especially benefits that you currently/last had). If a move is required, add all potential relocation benefits. **ALWAYS NEGOTIATE THAT TAXABLE RELOCATION BENEFITS ARE BUMPED UP TO COVER THE TAXES!**

In your second column, list the worth of any benefits that you currently have or had. Examine the list in your third column and list what value is minimally acceptable for you. Finally, the other columns are your offers.

This spreadsheet enables you to compare your offers to ensure your needs are covered — and you are comparing your offers equally.

| Compensation/Benefits | Current/Last | Minimum Acceptable | Company Offer |
|---|---|---|---|
| Salary | | | |
| Sign On Bonus | | | |
| Performance Bonus | | | |
| Stock Options | | | |
| Equity | | | |
| Health Insurance | | | |
| Dental Insurance | | | |
| Vision Insurance | | | |
| PTO | | | |
| Vacation | | | |
| Sick Leave | | | |
| 401(k) | | | |
| Pension | | | |
| Flexible Schedule | | | |
| Work From Home | | | |
| High Speed Internet | | | |
| Laptop/Desktop | | | |
| Phone | | | |
| Cell Phone | | | |
| Gym Membership | | | |
| FMLA | | | |
| Car | | | |
| Public Transportation | | | |

This spreadsheet was passed along to us by Pat Mencimer of Park City, UT when we conducted our Park City Career Network meetings from 2009 to 2016.

**By the way, continue networking and interviewing throughout your salary negotiation process. A better offer with another company may**

**be generated — and being totally transparent may add leverage to your negotiation with both companies.**

Your job is to continue networking even after you start with a new company. Until both sides are happy with your offer, it is not done. One or the other side may step away from the negotiations. Therefore, keep networking until you start your first day. At this point, you are saying, "I should keep networking after we negotiated an offer that I accepted?" Yes. You cannot control the economy nor Covid-19 nor terrorist attacks nor other potential impacts on a company. Candidates have called me the day they were supposed to start with a new company, only to discover the company suffered a downturn and could not hire them on their start date. Generally, that does not happen at the executive level because of potential lawsuits, but I have seen it happen several times at mid-level and technical positions.

In Step 1, I covered taking stock of your skills. Later, we discussed the importance of including your impacts in your resume and interview. This is the time for you to review your professional list of accomplishments for reinforcement during your salary negotiations.

> I met with the President and the COO of one of my recruiting clients. We discussed a senior position in detail. When we discussed the value of the position, they gave me a compensation range. This is their target. Based on my talent attraction experience, if the perfect candidate with all of the preferred experience interviews well, executives are sometimes able to flex on their top budget number.

This is a good time to remind you that a company places a certain value on a position. You may feel you may be worth more or need more, but to that company, the position is worth only what they budgeted — or possibly slightly more, based on the story above. Many times, people have shared with me that their spouses wanted to be stay-at-home parents, and therefore they "needed" more money. Your financial situation is not the company's issue. It is yours.

Do not begin that conversation with a representative of the company or your recruiter. That discussion raises questions on your judgment. Do not attempt to present your problems as their problems. In case you have not put two and two together, I have had that conversation more times in 40 years on the recruiting side than you want to know.

Some companies will require a candidate to put compensation requirements in a cover letter when a resume is submitted. This is one of their screens. The third question I ask every candidate is their salary requirement to see whether I feel their expectations are "reasonable." After so many years in the recruitment industry, I generally have a pretty good feel for the current salary ranges for most positions. In this Step, you will learn how to handle those compensation/salary requests.

Let's continue to discuss compensation conversations. If you were contributing at a high level within a large company, you may be surprised how the value may change in a smaller company. In some smaller companies, your value may be substantially higher. Whereas in another company, they may feel that you were over-compensated. You may feel it is a minefield out there; however, there are ways to navigate/manage through it.

Now would be a good time to read Alina Tugend's column in *The New York Times* — "Job Hunting's Delicate Dance" — where we discuss salary negotiations: http://www.nytimes.com/2012/07/28/your-money/job-huntings-delicate-dance-shortcuts.html

Many companies do not understand that recruiting is sales. You can use that to your advantage. Most recruiters do not want to waste their time. A growing trend among states is to make the question of your current earnings illegal. If they ask you what you seek in this new job, respond by asking *"What is the compensation/salary/hourly range for this position?"*

Many times, their response will save everyone time. Simply put, if the company does not value the work produced by this position, you either have a wonderful opportunity to prove them wrong or you may experience many frustrating days if your work is not valued.

> Recently, I received a call from a recruiting firm asking if I would be interested in a contract recruiting consulting assignment in Omaha. I said, "Sure." Then I asked the hourly rate the client was willing to pay. She replied, "$17.50 per hour." I chuckled and told her I had not worked for so little since the 1970s. Obviously, they did not value talent acquisition very highly. If you pay for a clerk, that is probably what you will get.

Negotiation is an art, not a science. Most importantly, remember not to take the negotiations personally. While I realize that it is personal to you and your family, remember that essentially you are "selling" your services to the new company; therefore, this is a business sales situation and objectivity is important. Do not be afraid to walk away from an offer that is too low. It is the wrong position for you. We do not work these long hours just to be frustrated in our jobs. If they do not value the position high enough to pay your worth, you will be frustrated almost daily because they will not enable you to produce your desired impacts.

## Let's Dive into Salary Negotiation!

Remember **CORE** from our last Step? It is time to apply it again in Salary Negotiation. This practice will earn you compensation increases, especially if you worked at the same employer for a long time.

**C — Confidence —** If you are not confident in your Salary Negotiating skills, now is the time to ACT Confident! Your confidence will reflect well on you, as it did in your interviews. If HR or someone on the interviewing team comments, "You are a Tough Negotiator." Confidently respond, "Would you agree that I will need to negotiate in this position?" They will say, "Yes." Then you respond "Wouldn't it be better for you to see my negotiating skills now (slight pause) before I come on board?" Let us face it — THAT is the purpose of interviews.

**O — Optimism —** Think about your current position. You have worked your way through the ENTIRE Process to this point. You know from previous Steps that the Manager is hoping that YOU are the person they hire! They selected you to negotiate compensation. Is there a Better Time to be Optimistic?

**R — Research —** Did the company give you the salary range of the position? Does the range meet your needs and create excitement for you? If it is slightly lower, we can fix that! The Total Compensation Package is important. Consider the Deferred Compensation — 401(k) match, profit-sharing, and other benefits.

**E — Execute —** You have your Confidence and Optimism where you need them. You know your compensation needs and desires. Now is time to use my script to EXECUTE on your Compensation negotiation. You Got This!

You now know when salary negotiation informally begins from both sides: the company side is when the position is budgeted; the candidate side is when you decide on the worth of the position.

When does salary negotiation formally begin? My feeling is when one side or the other begins to discuss money. There are three places a company may begin that conversation:

1. If a recruiter calls you and asks to have a conversation with you (it is my third question on my phone interview).
2. When a candidate applies online, companies generally will inquire what you seek. Human resources asked the engineers who developed the candidate tracking systems to require that candidates write a number instead of writing "negotiable" or "open." They use the "salary requirement" response to screen out candidates who seek too high a level of compensation AND too low a level of compensation. Interestingly, this practice perpetuates the gender wage gap because a woman who is earning 10% to 15% less than her male counterpart, is not comfortable "requiring" as much as the male who is earning more.
3. When you meet in person, if the company has not asked before now, this will likely be one of the first questions to kick off the interview.

Would you like the "Humbert Hack" to avoid putting a number in the space? Simply write the number 1 as your salary requirement. When the clerk asks you what you seek, this is your script:

**"Would you agree that job descriptions rarely describe the job, and my resume was tuned to reflect your job description so I would be selected for an interview? Therefore, it probably does not accurately describe my skills and experience relative to your job. Doesn't it make sense to discuss the job and my experience and skills before we discuss compensation? Would you agree if I like you and you like me, we will find some middle ground?"**

As the person who created that script, I smile when the candidate uses that script on me. I may test their resolve with an "Awww c'mon!" Stick to your guns! You may at this point simply ask for the range. If it is sufficient, say "My requirements are in that range."

Generally, you will be past the initial hurdle at that point. Never give a number this early in the conversation — except (There is ALWAYS an Except!) if the recruiter is a third-party recruiter. Then they may require you to give them your compensation requirements ahead of your introduction to their client. Ask them to give you their best guess of your value after they interview you. They may suggest more than you were thinking. At that point, you have a decision. The better recruiters will try to negotiate more for you because that is how they are paid — a percentage of total compensation for the first year (typically).

If you successfully pass this test, you will meet with the manager. Human resources will let them know that you did not give them your desired compensation target.

Before I go through the salary negotiation script with you, understand that while it has been proven effective for candidates for more than three decades, when dealing with people and their emotions, nothing works 100 percent of the time. Pay attention not only to what the other person says but how they say it. If you sense they are not receiving it well, you may need to change your direction or decide that you may not want to work with them. Too often, a young and inexperienced human resources representative may be defensive. The seasoned HR executive generally will be fine.

If you are an executive, you may be negotiating with either the board of directors or the executive management team. They understand how to negotiate and probably will be a little disappointed if you do not try to negotiate a better package.

> One of the CEOs that I work with often, once commented to me after a vice president of sales accepted their offer. "I wish they had negotiated a little tougher. They will need to do so for our benefit. It would have been nice to see how he performed."

**When the manager asks you for your compensation requirement, this is your script —**
**"Until we discuss the position and truly know:**

- **what the job entails;**
- **what you expect from me;**
- **what positive, measurable impacts I can make; and,**

• **where I can grow within the company over the next five years, I cannot make an intelligent assessment on a fair level of compensation. Let us move on with the interview so we can get those questions answered."**

In 2008, I coached a CFO in Boston in his search. His response may give you a sense of his age. After I gave him this script, he replied, *"If a CFO interviewed with me and did not know what the job entailed and what I expected from him, do you know what he would feel next? My foot in his ass!"*

I said that is fair. *"Do you mind if I ask you a couple of questions? Based on what you said, you probably agree that the CFO of General Motors does the exact same work as a CFO at an early-stage startup?"*

*No.*

*"Okay mind if I ask you another question? Are you saying that the CFO of a highly profitable medium-sized firm does the exact same work as the CFO of a corporate turnaround?"*

*"You win."*

All companies are different.

Isn't that script correct? Without that information and understanding of the challenges and potential impacts, how do you assign a compensation number to a position? Additionally, you need to get a sense of how the company values this position. Their offer will tell you where they value this position. The script works! These are two examples recently during the Covid-19 pandemic:

> I received a call from a Director of IT whom I was coaching who was excited to tell me he just accepted a position with a new company, after being laid off from his previous employer. He followed our script perfectly. He was also able to negotiate with two companies because he kept networking while one company took its time to develop an offer. This client negotiated an offer as a Global VP of IT with compensation well into six figures (10% increase over his previous salary), with bonuses and full relocation. He accepted his offer and started during Covid-19. During the "stay safe, stay home" Covid-19 directive, smart companies continue to hire!

And recently, an experienced gentleman I coached used this script as he interviewed for a project manager position. He was amazed that since he followed the negotiating script, his offer was 35% above his current base and with the targeted bonus, if it pays out, will earn him over 40% more. The company was so excited to recruit him (he networked into the company), that they extended an offer three hours after his interview ended!

During your interview, it is important to get an agreement on where they feel you may be able to make measurable impacts. Make note of these on a separate page in your notepad.

Once your interview is over, the manager or board member may say, "Now you know what the job entails, what we expect from you, where you may be able to make impacts, and where you may be able to grow within the next five years. What is your assessment of a fair level of compensation?"

Would you agree that most people like to be appreciated? Of course, they do! The manager who asks what your compensation assessment after the interview, is giving you a buying signal. Therefore, you respond in kind. If you are truly interested in the position, your response should follow these lines:

"I am very interested in your position because of what the job entails (mention two or three requirements about what the job entails that are attractive to you) and what you expect from me (mention two or three aspects that excite you). Can we chat briefly about the potential impacts I can make?" Here, go over your list of agreed impacts, reinforcing that you are an impact performer. Finally, discuss the positive side of potential future growth.

Then say,

"It is not good for me to come into an organization at too high a level of compensation, nor is it good for me to come into an organization at too low a level. **I am very interested in this position. Please make me the best offer that you can, and I will sincerely consider it.**"

This gives you a salary-negotiation strategy. The first party that puts a number on the table loses negotiation leverage. You have not negotiated a salary yet. You have only negotiated whether you will be the first party to put a number on the table.

**This script enables you to push salary negotiation where it belongs — when both parties indicate an interest in each other.**

As I mentioned in Step 9 on "Impassioned Interviewing," once you get 15 to 20 minutes from your interview, sit down in a quiet place and jot down your "Wish I Would Have Saids." These are the better examples of your experience and past impacts that you should have used during the interview. They may be introduced in your salary negotiation if an offer is extended.

After a successful interview where both sides indicate interest in each other, you may receive a call to return so they can extend you an offer in person. Or they may choose to call you to extend an offer over the phone. Different companies handle offers in different ways. If a third-party recruiter is involved, the recruiter strongly prefers to extend the offer. Sometimes, a human resource professional will extend the offer. In other companies, the hiring manager makes the call to extend an offer.

Many times, companies will extend a contingent offer prior to completing their due diligence of reference checking, background check, credit check (normally only for executives and employees who handle money), and drug test results. The offer is contingent upon the successful completion of those items.

Up until now, have we negotiated a salary? No. We have just negotiated whether you would tell them your salary requirements and created a foundation for your interview.

When you receive your offer, if you are going to try to negotiate a higher base, bonus, options, higher relocation benefits, etc., now is the time to say, **"Thank you! I am very interested in this position and the opportunity to work with you. Do you have any flexibility in your offer?"** There will probably be one of two answers.

They may say something along the lines of, "You asked us to give you our best offer. This is it." Now you have a decision to make. Is this the right position and the right company for you?

As we covered earlier, however, they may say, "Why do you ask?" If they ask that question, the door is cracked open for you to reply, **"I am very interested in this position and working with you (or the manager or** board). I was hoping for a larger package. Additionally, while I was reviewing our conversation, there were a few examples that better demonstrate the impacts I could make here. Could we spend a few minutes chatting about them?"

If you are asking for additional compensation, remember it is a good idea to give the company additional information on which to base their decision. Otherwise, it is very easy for them to say that their compensation decision was based on the information you gave them.

Companies typically will not increase the base compensation of their offer by a large percentage because they do not want to negatively impact their compensation ranges. They do have other ways to increase your compensation for this year, particularly if you must accept a cut in your base.

The first way a company may supplement your base income is to offer a signing bonus. This allows you to earn the same or more than you did at your last job without impacting their base compensation. Next budget year, they can decide to raise the compensation bands or give you a promotion (if deserved). Generally, the signing bonus is given on your first day. Some companies will hold all or a portion of your bonus until you work past the probationary period.

Another way that companies can add income is by adding a week or more of paid vacation to your package. If you were in your previous position for a long time, it is expected (by some companies) that you will ask for more vacation to match your previous number of days. This is a particularly attractive alternative for people who like to travel or treasure their days off. The key is to take the time off.

Some companies will offer quarterly and annual bonuses. When I worked for a startup as a manager, I was constantly amazed when I was paid a bonus and the company was not showing a profit; however, I did accept the check. These bonuses generally are based on the individual and the company hitting certain measurable targets.

Depending on your position, some companies will offer a car. Again, just understand the potential tax impact. The Internal Revenue Service considers the lease value as income.

Finally, if moving is required, the relocation package may be an area that can have a positive impact on your decision. Few companies are willing to buy houses these days, at least at a price that people are willing to accept. If the position requires relocation, it would be wise for you to visit the CNNMoney Salary Comparison site (www. money.cnn.com/calculator/pf/cost-of-living/index.html) to compare how far your current salary will go in another city. There are companies that offer spousal job dearch assistance  (I have provided that service many times for my clients and their candidates). Your findings may impact your decision or even give you a stronger negotiating platform.

Remember, we are speaking of a compensation package. The package may contain elements that are focused on your situation. A phrase that may be utilized is if you could offer (i.e., a bonus that will cover the difference in your 401(k) or 403(b) match, health insurance for my spouse and I) it will make me whole.

> One of my executive career coaching clients received an offer in another large city. His desire was to remain in his current home and work from home and commute to the company headquarters when needed rather than relocate. I showed him the CNN Salary Calculator. When he used the CNN Money Salary Calculator, he found the company could save money by paying for his travel rather than paying any relocation costs. He showed the CNN Salary Calculator to the company and they agreed.

Many people are not able to sell their house at the house's current appraised value. So, there is a loss *before* you move. Perhaps you could negotiate the appraised fair market value of your current home with the difference reimbursed to you. Or, you may be able to compensate for this loss in other areas of your relocation package — possibly have the company pack and move you instead of just moving you. Also, remember that not all expenses are deductible for income tax purposes. You may negotiate that the company increases your relocation package to cover the difference in the loss from income taxes.

> Once we were packed by a moving company. I made the bad mistake of leaving my suitcase with my clothes for the trip and my next day at the office in my bathtub. I told three people not to pack it. When someone called me out to our garage to ask if we were taking or leaving something, my suitcase

must have fit perfectly in a box. When I returned, the suitcase was packed — and probably already on the truck. Next time, anything that I do not want to be packed will be in my car before the movers arrive. I had to buy clothes, toiletries, and an inexpensive duffle to get through the next two days.

**Your move will be easier if your children are also "recruited" to the new area.**

If you are moving middle school or high school-age children, ask the new company if the children can accompany you on your first or second house-hunting trip. The children may yell and scream regarding the move, but they are more flexible than you give them credit. They just want some say in their move; therefore, set up meetings with principals or curriculum specialists and coaches, drama teachers, music teachers, (any other special-interest professionals) before your house-hunting trip. In your request for the meeting, coach the individual to address the children, not you. Set these meetings to give them a choice of school districts if you can. Then look for housing in the school district the children select. When we moved from Maryland to Iowa, we followed this practice. While our daughters (going into junior year of high school and 7th grade) were not happy, their sports teams welcomed them — and made the transition easier.

If your spouse works and will need to find a job in the new area, ask for job-search help for your spouse. It can be formal or informal help. Depending on your spouse, networking may be difficult in a new area. Any introductions your company can make will certainly help with their acceptance of the move.

During the same move that I described previously in this chapter; my wife interviewed at two hospitals in the new city during our house-hunting trip. It gave her a sense of the area and her potential employment opportunities. After returning to Maryland, she received an offer from one of those hospitals. Her acceptance of that offer made her feel better about our move. And, YES, she did follow my advice on negotiating!

Therefore, your salary negotiations may include the request for benefits that you have not considered. Caution: if you are really interested in this job, pick and choose the benefits or increases that you need. Do not just run the checklist of all of them at the same time.

If the company gets the sense you are just interested in taking an offer to your current company to receive a counteroffer, do not be surprised if they rescind theirs. As a professional recruiter, it is easy to tell when a candidate is shopping to receive a counteroffer from their current firm. Suddenly, they begin to make excuses to avoid making commitments to start — or they stop returning calls.

# IMPORTANT!

**Review the total Salary Negotiation Script from the first conversation with the company until you negotiate a better package. Practice it until it is part of you. Remember, your income and benefits are dependent upon a successful negotiation.**

What a nice segue to the next Step, "Resignation Rewards." In this television interview, I discussed how to handle counteroffers and we'll dig deeper into this topic in the next Step: — https://www.youtube.com/watch?v=y4qJWd7-bt8

First, let's review our checklist for the salary-negotiation process for people who are truly interested in the position.

**First! Let us CELEBRATE! If you are reading this Step, you are nearing or have received an offer!** Always celebrate your successes! Adding interviewing and strong salary negotiation skills adds many threads to your tapestry brand. It is part of you.

# Job-Search Process Checklist — Art of Salary Negotiation

☐ You continue to network until your first day on the new job. There is no need to tell the people with whom you are networking that you expect an offer. Networking remains the same. Continue to interview. You never know if an offer will be rescinded because of a sudden company downturn or the new company suddenly finds a better qualified candidate than you. These new people become part of your larger network once you start any new position. **For professionals who decide to take charge of their career, the first months of new employment**

**are just a pause in your networking as you learn your new posi-
tion — inside or outside your current company.**

▢ You review your list of "Wish I Would Have Saids" that you created after your interviews.

▢ When an offer is extended, the first thing you should do is tell them you are interested in the job and in working with them. Then you may either accept their offer if you are happy with it or ask if they have some flexibility in the offer.

▢ If they have some flexibility, ask if you can discuss your new information (Wish I Would Have Saids) that may impact their offer.

▢ Assure them that you are very interested in their position and working with them.

▢ It is important to negotiate your offer with them in a positive fashion. Do not take these negotiations personally.

▢ Discuss various options with them regarding increased base compensation, signing bonus, quarterly and annual bonuses, stock or stock options, increased vacation time, relocation benefits, education benefits, relocation benefits (if appropriate). Keep in mind the benefits that some companies have that differentiate themselves from other companies.

▢ When you are happy with your negotiations, be prepared to accept their final offer immediately and commit to the start date. I hope the information presented here helps you in your negotiations!

## Remain Positive!

"People do what you expect them to do . . ."
Morgan Wootten,
Hall of Fame Basketball Coach

Good luck!

*It is time to excitedly head to*

## STEP 11 —
## RESIGNATION REWARDS!

*I AM A PROFESSIONAL.*
*I GOT THIS!*

# EXPECT SUCCESS!

# *RESIGNATION REWARDS!*

Congratulations! You received an acceptable offer and your creative juices are beginning to flow. If you were a victim of a layoff, you are even more excited — and you do not have to worry about a resignation.

The Science of Psychology continues to play in your resignation since it is well known that many people resist change. Making a career change is often difficult for that very reason.

If you are employed, and many of you are, read on! This is about to get interesting. We will discuss your resignation — and *ta dumm!* — the inevitable counteroffer.

End your tenure in your current employer in a positive fashion. Many times (unfortunately) former managers remember you more for how you left their company than for your time working there — truly a paradox. They did not appreciate your contributions while you were there, and suddenly when you are poised to leave, they gain a sudden interest in your talents.

As a professional with 15, 20, 30 or more years of experience, you are looking around your office and mentally remembering the good times. Sometimes, you wonder what if you had a more effective manager? What if you worked at a company that valued your service? You could have grown as they promised when they hired you. The lack of these elements were the motivations to leave. Remember them. In my experience, money is a factor but not the driving factor when you decide to leave.

Your resignation is a process and a promise. You may not have ever thought of resignations as such. You may have thought of resignation as, "I quit." The process of a resignation includes the potential counteroffer. Some shortsighted professionals tend to use resignations as their way to get a raise. Not smart. Sooner or later, the manager will simply accept their resignation — they better have an excellent position lined up!

The best way to resign is to write a resignation letter. It needs to be simple, positive and clear. It is also a way for you to avoid the initial potential conflict. Generally, managers will absorb the fact that you are resigning before coming to you to ask questions about your resignation.

## This is a sample resignation letter:

Date

Dear *Manager* (obviously, use their name):

I want to thank you for the time that I have spent working with you. This has been a time of personal and professional growth for me. *Company Name* (your current employer) is a great company; however, I have received and accepted an offer to work with another great company. This new position helps me further my professional goals, and I am looking forward to starting with them on (start date).

My last day with *Company Name* will be Friday, Month Day (two-weeks notice). During the next two weeks, I will transition any uncompleted work to co-workers.

The decision to leave is a final decision for me. I have no interest in receiving a counteroffer.

Sincerely,

(your signature)

John Doe

As you can see, the information is concise and positive. There is no need to share the name of your new employer.

**When asked why you are leaving, simply say the new position is with a company that allows you to grow and make new impacts — and that you are really looking forward to working with the new company.**

Your manager needs to know that you are happy with your decision to leave and will not consider a counteroffer. Tell your manager if he/she has any transition questions after your departure, you are willing to answer any of those questions.

If the manager pushes you to stay longer than two weeks to transition your work, remember any additional time in the position may be very painful when they pressure you to accept a counteroffer — and they will pressure you almost daily. I have worked with candidates who called me in their third week. They were complaining to me that it was not about transitioning work. The company was pressuring them to stay. I suggested that the next day the person announce, "The transition is completed, so I am leaving at noon to start with my new company. It has been a pleasure working with you! Thank you!"

As your performance was measured during your tenure with that company, your performance as you depart will be measured and remembered. Make it as positive a memory as you can.

Emotions run high when you resign. So, there is no surprise when someone tells me they have decided to accept a counteroffer within their own company.

Before accepting a counteroffer, you should attempt to make it a rational decision rather than an emotional decision. Consider that a recruiting industry newsletter like the *Fordyce Letter* and online recruiting sites such as https://www.ere.net/ track the percentages of people who accept counter offers and are still with their company six months to a year later.

**An amazing 87 percent of all people who accept a counteroffer leave their current company within a year after accepting the counteroffer to stay. Of the 87% who leave in a year, 67% are gone in the first 6 months. Those are staggering statistics!**

Think about that for a minute. Las Vegas was built and all that electricity is paid for by people taking risks when the odds are against them; therefore, of every 1,000 who accepted counteroffers, 130 people remain at their company a year later, while 870 of them have left (some of those not by their choice), usually within six months.

The 870 people who left must experience the stress of another job search — and usually have one fewer option since they have broken that trust. Because they were successful enough to receive an offer this time, they should be confident enough to succeed again. There is no reason to believe the original position is still open — or if the company even would consider them as a candidate again. The original trust has now been broken by acceptance of the counteroffer.

Professionals who decided to take control of their careers are focused on their careers. Their decisions to move on are generally rational growth decisions, not one that was made during an emotional state. Therefore, once they make their decisions to leave — and then, accept new positions — those decisions are final.

I worked with a candidate who was interested in a management position within a consulting company in the top-secret world. My client was a small boutique consulting company within that world that had a great reputation with its clients. As a result, they were beginning to grow and needed to bring in a technically talented manager to help that growth succeed.

The candidate sailed through the interviews successfully. He had the perfect credentials for my client and the right attitude and skills to manage a small team. As a result of his interviews, the candidate received an offer from my client. When he resigned, his current company offered him a counteroffer that matched his newly offered compensation from my client. More importantly, they offered him the opportunity to lead a team. Since he viewed himself as a loyal employee and his company appeared to match my client's offer, he accepted his company's counteroffer.

My client was very disappointed on several levels:

1. *They thought their search for a new manager was over and that he would soon start.*
2. *Once they extended his offer and he accepted, they assumed their search was over and notified other candidates.*
3. *Now they were going to have to begin from scratch to search for a new qualified candidate within a very small community of potential candidates.*
4. *He had broken the trust and the commitment that he made to my client.*

You can probably understand why my client did not want to hear his name later.

And later did come . . . After he accepted the counteroffer, his manager told him that they would begin to expand in several months and that is when he would get the team to manage. As soon as his company heard that a new manager began at my client's company three months later, they told him that they were slowing down their expansion and he would not have a team to manage for the foreseeable future.

Of course, he did still have the extra compensation, but the reason he was looking initially was not money, it was the additional challenge of managing a team. Now he was unhappy again — and his own company broke that trust, again. He immediately called me as soon as his manager gave him that news. "Was the position still available?" I told him that my client just had someone start in the position the day before.

Now he realized that his company had betrayed him and was more disappointed than before he began his first search. My client was not interested in hearing he was available because they felt he broke his commitment to them. He found another position a short time later and left his company. It is not always that simple, especially in small worlds like the top-secret worlds. The word gets out.

## Why Do Managers and Companies Extend Counteroffers?

As a talent attraction expert, it is always interesting to me how many managers do not understand the unexpected consequences of treating a direct report poorly — until that person decides to resign. Suddenly, all the reasons they need to be nice and try to recruit that person to stay floods their minds.

There are many reasons they try to become "friends" again:

1. They really need a person to fill that role, and the current person did

so nicely (and sometimes below market value, particularly if they have been a long-term employee).

2. They also recognize no other current employee can fill that role.

3. They suddenly recognize the value that the person brings, particularly the knowledge of the position and potential competitive intelligence that person will take with them.

4. The manager recognizes he or she will now need to conduct a search for a new employee and spend the time and money to train them.

5. If they leave, someone else will need to perform those tasks until the position is filled by a new person and they are trained.

6. Some people are poor managers. They may have already lost members of their team and are afraid of how this next departure will impact their future as a manager.

7. They are also afraid that this departure, particularly if the person is well-liked, may trigger more employees to look for and find new positions.

8. They are afraid of the impact of the employee's departure on morale.

9. They are afraid of the impact of hiring someone new to their compensation structure, particularly if the current employee discovered the compensation was under market value.

10. They simply decided that they did not want the competition to have your skills.

Most of the time, concerns revolve around themselves and not their employees. These managers are struggling to maintain their grip on a person who stated he or she is leaving. Suddenly, an employee who was not so important has become a very important person (for a while).

Those are some of the reasons and fears of the manager and the company.

# Why Should an Employee Be Wary of the Counteroffer?

1. Now, your manager and company know you are unhappy there. So, a certain level of trust has been broken within your own company.

2. What are your most important assets to your company now that they know you want to leave? Your knowledge of your position, processes,

systems, people, etc. Some of this knowledge may not be replaced for a long time.

3. If they offer you more money during the counteroffer, are you setting yourself up to lose next year's raise? This should be a 'real concern' as this happens much more than one would think — especially if the counteroffer happens in the 2nd half of a budget year.

4. Why are you suddenly worth more today — after your resignation — than you were worth yesterday? Many people become upset when they consider this aspect.

5. Is there a possibility your company will conduct a brain drain on you after you accept a counteroffer? They know the statistics of how fast you will leave. Will they get the information they need from you and then replace you through a reorganization once a new person is up to speed? I can answer that question — YES! I have seen it happen many times.

6. Remember when we discussed the premise of behavioral interviewing? When backed into a corner, this manager will treat you the same as before your resignation. Especially if you accept the counteroffer because they feel like they have you locked in with no place to go.

7. Do you really believe them when they say they are happy you decided to stay? Are they happy for you, or happy for themselves? Now they have "Old Reliable" still in the seat and do not have to spend time and money to recruit a replacement.

8. Remember the odds are against success at your company after you resign from that company. They just want someone to do the job until they decide how to "protect themselves" — probably with your replacement. You may even be asked to train that person.

While I preach a good game on counteroffers, it took two bad experiences for me to be convinced that accepting a counteroffer is unwise.

I was a senior recruiter working with a noted contingent recruiting firm (fee based or Head Hunter) with offices in Washington, D.C., and New York City. I was successful in the contingency world. I decided that I wanted to mentor and train my own team. There were some practices I wanted to do differently than my manager.

After discussions with my manager/partner broke down, I discussed my candidacy with another firm in Maryland a little closer to my home. They made me an offer immediately and I accepted.

When I went back to my manager/partner and resigned, he was dumbfounded. He went on a full-court press to get me to stay, including putting me on a shuttle flight to New York City to visit with his partners. His partners wined and dined me and assured me that we would come to an agreement and I would be able to develop my team. I returned that evening full of promise and decided to stay there. The other firm was very disappointed that I changed my mind.

Over the next couple of months, I focused primarily on my recruitment fee production while looking for the right talent to recruit. About the time I found someone to hire, the partner had hired someone else to grow his consulting business and told me that it was up to the new manager. The new manager told me that he wanted to go in another direction (consulting). The trust was broken. I left two weeks later.

I am still friendly with my manager/partner there. He acknowledged that he made a bad decision — and so did I. Once I decided to leave the first time, I should have left.

When you resign, what should you expect to hear from your company if they are going to extend a counteroffer? Many times, I list the following statements for the candidates and ask them to tell me how many they hear. While this is an important time for the departing employee, companies are amazingly consistent in what they say to the person who wants to leave.

1. "I am shocked that you want to leave. I thought you were happy. As a matter of fact, tomorrow we were going to discuss a (promotion, raise, new project, etc.) with you." (Call me a cynic, but the supposed timing is an amazing coincidence, wouldn't you agree?)

2. "You are a very valuable employee. We need to see what we can do to encourage you to stay." (SUDDENLY you are recognized as valuable! Truly? What about all the years you worked there?)

3. "I am happy that you came to me because I planned to chat with you about moving to another organization in our company (that was nixed in previous conversations weeks before)."

4. "I am very disappointed that you chose such a busy time to leave our organization. Can't you see the impact your departure will have on everyone else?" (I love this one. The manager is trying to put a guilt trip on you.)

5. "Your manager just came to me to discuss your resignation. I asked if I could talk with you. You are a key person in our growth plans. I am sorry we have not shared this with you sooner. Let's sit down and discuss the needed changes . . ." (Generally, an executive speaking. If you accept a counteroffer, how soon will you see the changes? Do not hold your breath . . .)

6. "What will it take for you to stay?" (At least that one is upfront in its intent!)

7. "As you know, we rarely give counteroffers here, but you are such a key person, we will make an exception. What do you want to stay?" (It is cheaper to give you that small raise than spend time and money to find someone new that has to be trained.)

8. "Thank you for coming to me and discussing the needed changes. Would you like to lead those changes?" (If you accept the counteroffer, the desire to make immediate changes in the organization dissolves shortly after you accept.) Then they will say, "Let's just finish what you are working on first. Then we will discuss the changes." (Note, they will not say "make the changes" again.)

For your own satisfaction, track how many of those statements you hear when you resign.

My client extended an offer to a candidate who accepted the offer. The candidate and I sat down. I chatted with him about the counteroffer experience that I had personally. Then we discussed the statements that he might hear the next day when he resigned. I suggested that he track them and call me at the end of the day and let me know which ones he heard.

Sure enough, I received a call from him early in the evening after they had taken him to dinner (those wily devils!). He was laughing. He thanked me for my counter-offer counseling. They managed to hit seven out of eight statements. That is certainly better than average! They must have read my website! He honored his commitment and went to work with my client.

I have another counteroffer story. In 1993, we were traveling across the country looking for candidates for a Midwestern city. One candidate I interviewed received an offer. This is his story.

We extended the offer to this candidate and he accepted on the spot. He was so excited to join my client!

On Wednesday before he was leaving the company, his manager called him in and put him on the spot. He was great at putting employees on guilt trips, and this one worked. I received an email from one of the managers I worked with saying that he accepted a counteroffer. I asked the manager if he wanted me to try to "save" him. He replied, "Please!"

I called the candidate and asked if we could sit down for a soda on Saturday afternoon when I was back in town. He said, "Sure."

When we sat down in a restaurant, we chatted for almost an hour over the soda (called "pop" in some regions of the U.S. or "Coke" in Atlanta) discussing what had happened. When he was finished, I asked him if he was happy that he accepted the counteroffer. He was undecided. I suggested that in my experience when I make a decision that feels right, it seems the weight of the world has left my shoulders. I observed that, based on our chat, it appeared that weight was still there. Then I asked him if he would like me to tell him how to resign and still make orientation on Monday. He said, "Sure."

He told me that his manager usually was in on Mondays by 7 a.m. I told him to get there at 6:30 a.m. and empty his cubicle. When 7 a.m. rolled around, go to the manager and say, "two weeks ago I turned in my notice. Last week you pressured me to stay. I didn't want to stay, but you pressured me, so I accepted your counteroffer. After thinking it over during the weekend, I decided to honor my commitment and go to work for my new company. Here are my keys and identification. I need to run to make the orientation." Then leave.

He asked me if he could take some time to think about it. I said, "Sure, just let me know tomorrow if you want to be in orientation Monday morning so I can send a note to let them know to expect you. As promised, he called me on Sunday and told me he would be in orientation.

He enjoyed the new company so well that he stayed for 20 years. We are still friends.

**Bottom line — you committed your acceptance to your new manager. Honor your commitment.**

- Congratulations! Your start date in your new career is quickly approaching! Celebrate your success! Now, you are prepared to take charge of your career — and interview internally or externally for your next career challenge! Your tapestry for this segment of your life is nearing its completion. Remember to continue to grow and add more threads.

# Job Search Process Checklist

### Resignation Rewards!

- ☐ Write a simple, positive resignation letter.
- ☐ When asked why you are leaving, simply say the new position is with a company that allows you the opportunity to grow and make new impacts — and that you are really looking forward to working with the new company.
- ☐ Tell your manager that you are not interested and will not consider a counteroffer.
- ☐ Assure the manager that you will ensure your work is transitioned to the team.

- If pushed to remain on the job longer than two weeks, carefully monitor progress on transitioning work. Once the pressure to accept a counteroffer is greater than the pressure to transition work, it is time to leave immediately.
- Read once more the odds against a successful tenure after accepting a counteroffer.
- Understand the reasons why companies suddenly decide to extend a counteroffer.
- Review the reasons why the employee should be wary of the counteroffer.
- Count how many of the counteroffer related statements you hear from managers and executives once the word gets out that you resigned.
- Once you accept an offer and give a start date, honor your commitment to start on that date.
- Professionals who take charge of their careers are decisive. Once you decide the time has come to move, the decision is made and the commitment to the new company is honored.

This is a good time to discuss your first few weeks on the new job in **Step 12: Outstanding Onboarding!**

By now, you and your mirror should be on pretty good terms! It is expecting your visits in the morning and evening. This may be a stressful time. In track, races are lost when runners fail to run through the tape. Continue to run through the tape.

------------------------------------

*I AM A PROFESSIONAL*
*I GOT THIS!*

------------------------------------

# EXPECT SUCCESS!

## STEP 12

# *OUTSTANDING ONBOARDING!*

You had a tough, grueling search. Landing in your new position feels great! You are about to meet a group of new teammates who were looking forward to your arrival over the past two weeks — and now you are here! As you are soaking in the excitement of your new team and your excitement to get started, you realize that your search has finally come to fruition. The feelings of gratitude swarm over you. Then you focus on your new manager and your new job. It is almost like you were set free!

As RecruiterGuy, may I suggest that while everything is fresh in your memory, it is time to prepare for your next search? Jot down what actions were successful for you during this search. What would you have done differently? Think of this as your "debriefing." Document your search for your own records while still fresh in your mind. Remember, you never know when you will be looking again. This is the professional you created to take charge of your career mindset. In my last book, we called it Employee 5.0. Remember the Sciences of Psychology and Sociology, and Computer Science impacted your search. As you begin to integrate with your new employer, the Science of Psychology applies as you meet and begin to interface with your team. The Science of Sociology applies as you begin to absorb and become a valuable member of the organization's culture. Computer Science requires that you learn the software and processes of your new company.

Through this journey we traveled together, you have woven a tapestry of your skills, experience, attributes, stories, and preferences to create a brand that is you. For many of you, all of these elements were in place simply waiting to be woven together. This tapestry should not be hung on a wall and forgotten. This tapestry, your brand, makes you stronger in every day-to-day activity as a sole contributor, team member, and executive. As companies must protect their brand, protect Your Brand. In the process of lifelong learning, as you experienced during your career search, add new skills and experience to contribute to your company. Make positive, measurable impacts — and have fun doing so.

Remember to thank everyone who helped you in your search and let them know where you are now working. Now that you have a business relationship, they may be a good source to contribute to solutions to problems confounding you, and you may be able to return the favor.

Continue to network with people to see how you can help them. Remember your experience as you went through the job-search process. If you receive a call from someone who is attempting to network the way to a new position, take the call. Without spending an inordinate amount of time use your experience to make suggestions and help them better focus their search. That is how you pay it forward and become a leader. Remember, you now have a huge list of potential people they can use to network. Not everyone on your list is good for someone else's search, but at least a few of them are. You may make a difference in a person's life.

Understand that some people are users. Remember the opera singer warming up? Me, me, me, me! Spend tiny amounts of time with them instead and focus on people who understand networking is a two-way street.

One hopes you made some new friends during this journey. Nurture those relationships. They need not involve social interaction. They can be a quick phone call or e-mail asking how the person is doing. Keep your information on LinkedIn up to date and check out their activities occasionally. You may be able to answer a quick question for them.

One of the areas that most people can improve is to track their impacts. You can review this information preceding your annual review with your manager or executive board. If you find yourself in another search, this information will be sitting in a file on your personal computer or tablet (not your business computer), instead of needing to be dredged up. Managers do not always track your impacts well (as you probably discovered before your last move). Therefore, it is your responsibility to track them. As you work through your quarterly or annual reviews, it is good to bring impacts up for discussion. This is not bragging. It is reinforcing in your manager's mind the problems that you are helping them solve.

As you work with your new manager, agree on 3-month, 6-month, 9-month, and 12-month goals for your coming year. This keeps you on track to fulfill the goals for the year. Ask your manager to introduce you to the people with whom you will need to interface to accomplish the goals.

It is advisable to make this an annual practice with each manager. During your quarterly reviews, you should discuss the goals completed. It also is a good platform to use when you need your manager to introduce you to someone new inside the company or to a vendor to meet your goal.

During these discussions, develop an agreement on opportunities you see for your group and the company. Keeping your focus on your goals and company goals is the best way to be viewed as a person who makes a difference within the company. Helping your manager accomplish their goals while accomplishing your goals is the vehicle to be viewed as a team player. If you build consensus with others in your company, it also is a great way to grow respect.

Once you have some credibility (by meeting your goals) with your manager, your goal-review time is a great time to discuss your future career goals. If your manager has a mentor type of relationship with you, she or he can be a great person to help position you for your next move.

Remember in Step 8 *Newly Networking* when I said networking can be a simple conversation that can benefit both sides? Doesn't this also work inside companies? You may not call it networking inside your company, but that is what it is.

Effectively networking within your company is a great way to be more effective in working with other staff and management. Networking within your company with other managers is a way to move within your company to gain new experience and make new impacts without taking time to look for a new job in another company. This is an effective practice to break down silos, where the only focus is on that one organization, within companies. This cross pollination of ideas benefits all organizations.

Remember the goal of having so much fun at work that at the end of the day you say, "Wow! This was so much fun that I can't believe today is already over — and they are paying me, too!" How do you reach that level of job satisfaction? You reach it by making positive, measurable impacts and having fun. Meet your goals and help others meet theirs.

As you are meeting your goals, look for "dirty jobs" that others are avoiding. In my experience, these dirty jobs have such a reputation of being time traps or are such a pain to do that they develop the reputation of being a monster. Tackle one of those jobs at a time from a lean process-improvement or Six Sigma focus that eliminates waste with continuous process improvement. What you may discover is that your fresh look at the task can help you suggest improvements at the level where other people don't mind joining you, or you eliminated waste and contributed directly to the bottom line. You also may decide to automate it so no one must do it again. You may discover it has outlasted its usefulness. Of course, before discarding information or deleting a task, confirm with your manager that it no longer needs attention.

People who successfully clean up the dirty jobs and make them efficient are the ones who succeed in companies.

Do we need a checklist at the end of this book? This one is easy:

- - - - - - - - - - - - - - - - - - - - - - - - - - - - - - - - - - - - - - - - - - -

### *Make IMPACTS and Have Fun!*

*Finally, why not?*

### *I AM A PROFESSIONAL!*
### *I GOT THIS!*

*And you have proven that you do!*
*Congratulations!*

- - - - - - - - - - - - - - - - - - - - - - - - - - - - - - - - - - - - - - - - - - -

# EXPECT SUCCESS!
## ACKNOWLEDGMENTS

My life has been blessed. I have followed many of my dreams and even a few of my fantasies. In the summer of 1969, after my sophomore year at Assumption University in Worcester, MA, I properly set a goal to hitchhike from Washington, D.C. to Los Angeles in five days. My strategy included recruiting a friend from Assumption. We received a ride from just north of Wichita, Kansas to Huntington Beach, California — and made it in five days. We arrived in LA two weeks after Manson's clan killed Sharon Tate and her friends.

Then we set a goal to hitchhike from LA to San Francisco in 24 hours. We received three rides from Huntington Beach to Santa Monica. While we were standing on Route 101 with our "Frisco" sign, four hippy chicks picked us up. They were very nice. They said they were living on a ranch in the mountains above LA. They had a leader who gave them drugs and they did fun things. You know who they referred to. I feel another book about the importance of proper goal setting may be on the way. I may also relate how I set a goal to hitchhike from Las Vegas to Boston in 24 hours — and made it in 12.5 hours.

Thank you to my wife, Linda! We have been married for more than 48 years. Unless you are an author too, it may be hard to fathom the crazy hours authors may choose to write. Over my last three books, there have been many nights when I woke at 2 or 3 AM. I laid there as my brain said, "I have some cool things for you to write — GET UP!" When I got up, Linda asked if I was okay. The code became, "The words have to get out!"

Our two daughters, Becky and Sarah, inspire me. They are married to wonderful men, Jason and Ryan. Our granddaughters Stori and Zoe are so special! This has been a hard year for our country and our world with Covid-19. The pandemic prevented us from seeing and hugging our daughters and families for over a year. Many of you have felt the same impact.

This was a sad year because I lost a very good friend, Andrea Sturken. You may recognize Andrea as my Radar O'Reilly on my MCI contract in this book. She timed me as I reviewed resumes. Then told me how much time I spent on my first pass on your resume. She valiantly fought cancer for 20 years. Sadly, Andrea left behind her amazing husband, Brett, and their daughter, Sarah. Rest in peace Andrea.

Thank you to my family of six brothers and sisters and their families! We support each other. At the same time, our sense of humor prevents anyone's head from getting too big, especially mine.

In his book, *TopGrading*, Dr. Brad Smart discusses how we develop our work ethic as teens. Since I decided to pay my way through DeMatha Catholic High School in Hyattsville, MD at age 12, my work ethic has never been in question. There are three teachers and my guidance counselor who made significant impacts in my life. Thanks to Father Mike who was my freshman biology teacher — and awakened an interest in science that never left me. Thank you Dr. Buck Offutt, who was an English teacher. Buck influenced many guys like me over the years at DeMatha. His English classes were always interesting. He sat on his desk — and made it popular before Robin Williams in *Dead Poets Society*. My guidance counselor, John Moylan, knew I would get up at 4 AM every morning to deliver *The Washington Post*. He recommended me to Assumption University and my work ethic got me there. Finally, a man who influenced me in so many ways was Morgan Wootten. Morgan was my freshman history teacher, my freshman home-room teacher, and a customer on my *The Washington Post* paper route. As such, he helped me pay my way through DeMatha. Morgan was the DeMatha basketball coach for 40 years — and was such an amazing coach that he was admitted to the Naismith Basketball Hall Of Fame as the winningest basket-ball coach of all time in 2000.

My professors at Assumption University in Worcester, MA were instru-mental in taking a teen and helping him become a man. Their influence was so important. Assumption University did not give me a scholarship (nor did my grades deserve one). I was determined that was where I wanted to go to college — and I paid my way there too. I called Dr. John Burke after my first book was completed and told him that "Slacker Humbert" finally wrote a book. He was one of my English professors who influenced my writing. When he read my book, he told me that I made his day — as he made mine. Thank you to Larry Riordan. He was the admissions director at Assumption — and gave me a job in the admissions office. Who would have guessed my recruiting training began in a work-study job?

Thank you to Tom Grondalski for his proofreading skills. We have been best friends since Tom moved to our neighborhood our sophomore year at DeMatha. It is so nice to have a lifelong friend — another one of my blessings. Thank you to his wife, Chris for allowing Tom to spend time with my books — and therefore, with you.

Thank you to Mark Sugarman for listening and creating the cover for our book. You may reach him here — www.msugarman.com

Special THANKS go to Daria Meoli, the skilled editor of our book! Daria toiled through a very tough year homeschooling her children while editing our book. I believe you will agree that she was super! Thank you, Daria! You may reach her here — Daria Meoli | LinkedIn

Thank you to Kevin Callahan! He is the Expert Paginator! His design was key to making our book design enjoyable to read. You may reach Kevin at http://www.bngobooks.com/

Back in December 2001, I was told I had kidney cancer. Renal Cell Cancer then was almost always life-threatening. Fortunately, my guardian angel lobbied God on my behalf — and discovered my cancer before it grew too large. Thank you to Dr. Ann Metzger for following up with tests to discover my cancer when it was small — and referred me to Dr. Neil Mittelberg, the skilled urologist who performed surgery and removed the tumor. Linda and I believe I am still here with you because of all of the companies I helped find the right people — and all of the impacts in people's lives I have made by coaching them to their next career.

Thank you, God, for my extra years to serve You by helping others!